YOUR GUIDE TO

BETTER

MOTIVATION

DISCOVER THE SECRETS TO BECOMING
MORE EFFECTIVE TOMORROW
THAN YOU ARE TODAY.

Volume 9

OF

THE EFFECTIVENESS GUIDE

BY

EDWARD J. MURPHY

Never STOP Learning!

WHAT OTHERS SAY ABOUT
The Effectiveness Institute

"I highly recommend the books from The Effectiveness Institute as texts for new leaders and a review for seasoned leaders - as a reminder of what they should be doing. These books are unique because they're replete with valuable information that you can actually learn today and use tomorrow. If you want to become absolutely essential to any organization, these books are for you."

- Dennis D. Cavin
Lieutenant General, US Army (Retired)
Vice President Army and Missile Defense Programs
Lockheed Martin, Corporate Business Development

"I recommend the books from The Effectiveness Institute because Ed Murphy doesn't theorize; he draws on his extensive experience from many years of service in the US Military and from working as an Executive Coach in Corporate America. His keen insights and practical advice make these books required reading for anyone trying to negotiate the maze of organizational chaos."

- Lee Lacy
Assistant Professor
US Army Warfighter Book
Command and General Staff College

"The books from The Effectiveness Institute will help you become more effective at work and in life. They will also help you unlock your potential and direct your team to greater success. I highly recommend these books."

- Lance Revo
Principal Engineering Design Specialist
Cyber Security at AREVA NP

I DEDICATE

THIS BOOK

TO

My Granddaughter,

TAEGAN LEIGH STERN

"Tae, I won't be around during your lifetime. But if I were, I would tell you exactly what's in this book. That's why I wrote it. May it help you and your posterity find true joy and enhance the quality of your life. You have so much to give. Make a difference in the lives of others by serving them in some meaningful way, and you'll be richly rewarded in this life and the next. Know that I am always with you! Much love always

Other Books From
THE EFFECTIVENESS INSTITUTE

Here are the eleven volumes from *The Effectiveness Institute*, one for each Core Competencies of Effectiveness:

VOLUME 1: The Power of FOLLOWERSHIP

VOLUME 2: The Power of DELEGATING

VOLUME 3: The Power of PLANNING

VOLUME 4: The Power of ORGANIZING

VOLUME 5: The Power of COMMUNICATING

VOLUME 6: The Power of PROBLEM-SOLVING

VOLUME 7: The Power of AWARENESS

VOLUME 8: The Power of TRAINING

VOLUME 9: The Power of MOTIVATION

VOLUME 10: The Power of CHARACTER

All the above books are available at *Amazon.com*

Never STOP Learning!

This page is intentionally left blank.

CONTENTS

PREFACE

I'm often asked, "What does the picture mean on the cover of your book?"

This picture is a metaphor for the dilemma young people face when coming from school to the world-of-work.

They're unprepared, do not have the right tools, the right motivation, nor any clue of what's most important to every employer on the planet.

The cover image shows a young man rowing a boat in the fog. If you look closer, you'll notice that the boat is too small for the person in it. You can tell because one side of the boat is dipping so low in the water that it's almost taking on water. You can also tell that he has little experience in a boat because the other side of the boat is way out of the water because his weight is not evenly distributed.

He is also rowing in dense fog. He cannot see where he's going. The further he gets from shore; he cannot turn around and head back because he has no idea from which direction he came.

Finally, since he's not wearing a flotation device, he's assuming he won't have to swim. You know where assumptions take you, right? He is totally unprepared.

He didn't plan his trip, nor is he prepared to deal with the consequences of what lies ahead. He is, or will soon be, lost and at the mercy of nature.

Such is the fate of young workers today.

In today's job market, there's a huge skills gap between graduation and the first day on the job. As a result, young people lack the job skills needed to "hit-the-ground-running" and find themselves in dead-end, menial, minimum-wage jobs, trading time for money just to put food on the table. And it will take them decades before they're effective enough to *add value* to any employer. What a waste!

How do I know that? I know it because I've spent 20+ years of my life as an executive coach, working with hundreds of business executives and small business owners, seeking the answer to this simple question:

Why are some people more effective than others?

What do they think, say, and do that made them more effective?

During that time, I was privileged to work with some of the most exceptional men and women in America. Through their example, I learned the true definition of effectiveness by documenting what they did, how they did it, and most importantly, how they made people feel. What you'll find here is the result of my years of research.

Today, my purpose in life is to help you navigate the world-of-work, maximize your true career potential, and become more effective and successful at work and in life.

ENJOY!

INTRODUCTION

"Optimism is the faith that leads to achievement.
Nothing can be done without hope and confidence. "
- Helen Keller

This book is about **MOTIVATION!**

Motivation is your ability to energize the invisible driving force in others that influences their behavior, improves their performance, and unleashes their potential.

Motivation is also one of these eleven Core Competencies of your effectiveness and success at work and in life.

Followership, Delegating, Planning, Organizing, Communicating, Problem-Solving, Decision-Making, Awareness, Training, Motivating and Character.

This book is for everyone in the workforce who reports to another person for their work assignments, including employees working for an employer and small business owners, entrepreneurs, and the self-employed working for customers, clients, or patients.

Simply stated, this book is for you regardless of your occupation, position, or level of authority.

You may not realize that *Motivation* is one the most powerful and underrated transferrable skills in business today.

However, you'll have your work cut out for you because many workers are not motivated to do anything more than the minimum. Instead, they do just enough to stay out of trouble as they trade time for money just to put food on the table.

There are no incentives for them to make their company's products or services better. Also, many managers and supervisors lack the skills needed to use positive and negative motivators effectively.

To become more effective, you'll need to understand how their emotions and behavior contribute to or detract from the quality of their work or their relationships with others.

To improve their performance and unleash their potential, you'll also need to know how to demonstrate appreciation, recognition, encouragement, active listening, empathy, moral courage, respect, kindness, emotional intelligence, assertiveness, sensitivity to others, and resilience.

And let's not forget how to keep the peace, resolve conflict, correct unacceptable behavior, serve their team, or protect their character – all of which are addressed in this book.

Without these abilities, you'll be wasting your career sitting on the sidelines, watching others move ahead while wondering why?

I speak from 24 years as a US Army Officer and 20 years as an Executive Coach in Corporate America in Seattle, San Diego, Kansas City, and Phoenix.

As an Executive Coach, I was blessed to work with some of America's most successful men and women, including hundreds of business executives, teams, and small business owners. I documented what they said, did, how they did it, what worked and what didn't. But, most importantly, I documented how they made people feel.

As a result, I learned that the most effective and successful people stood out because they were able to do these two things better than anyone else:

- First, to consistently produce excellent results.

- Second, to add value to those who helped produce those results.

This book will enhance your ability to do both.

The fact is that you may be the top producer, but if you haven't added value to those who helped you, especially your boss, you'll never become effective or successful, period.

What new skills or abilities have you acquired in the last twelve months? What contributions have you made to your current position since this time last year?

And, most of all, what are you doing about it?

This book is unique because it:

- Gives you the most actionable tactics, techniques, and tools needed to consistently produce excellent results.

- Teaches you the best practices used every day by the most effective and successful people in their field, which you were never taught in school.

- Provides you with step-by-step instructions explaining what and how things should be done that you won't find anywhere in academia or Corporate America to help you maximize your true potential.

- Contains everything you want to know about *Motivation*, plus everything you didn't realize you need to know about how *Motivation* enhances your effectiveness and success in business.

I know that by learning, using, and sharing the best practices found here, you'll be well on your way to becoming more effective and successful.

Remember, no matter how good you think
you are; you can always be better.

So, what are you waiting for? You have too much to lose by not taking a more active role in your Professional Development.

When you're ready to *elevate-your-game* to the next level, join us on this incredible *Journey of Discovery.*

Also, if you feel this information could help someone else, please let them know. If it turns out to make a difference in their life, they'll be forever grateful to you, as will I.

Never STOP Learning!

Ed

Founder of *The Effectiveness Institute*

email: ed.murphy77@gmail.com

Stop wishing you were better and do something about it today!

1
THE POWER OF
MOTIVATION

*"In serving each other, we become free. May God give us
the wisdom to discover the right, the will to choose it,
and the strength to make it endure."*
- Sean Connery (as King Arthur), 1st Knight

This book will give you a far better understanding of *Motivation*, its definition, importance, and how to do it successfully.

Motivation is your ability to energize the invisible driving force in others that influences their behavior, improves their performance, and unleashes their potential.

Motivation is the driving force that keeps you going and comes from intrinsic (within) and extrinsic (external) sources. It provides the will to do what's necessary and aligns and elevates member drives to team goals. Motivating others requires an understanding of the needs and desires of others.

The secret to your success is to have a profound dose of inspiration with a double dose of motivation.

Here, you'll learn to use the most actionable *tactics, techniques, and tools* needed to master the *Art of Motivation*. As an executive coach for over 20 years, I know what your boss and customers expect, especially regarding your effectiveness and success at work.

Effective people know that their ability to motivate others is critical to their effectiveness and success at work. By learning, using, and sharing these *best practices*, you'll be well on your way to becoming the one person who adds the greatest value to the team - making you essential.

Also, to make this book easier to understand, I'll use the term "boss" instead of leader, employer, or customer. I do this because if you're an employee, your boss is your employer. And if you're self-employed or a small business owner, your boss is your customer, client, or patient.

This means that you'll always be working for a boss -
whoever pays you for your products or services.

This also means that you'll always be a follower of
someone - whoever pays you for your work.

So, let's get to work! Effective people know how critical motivation is to the success of their team.

Inspiration is what gets you started -
anything that moves you to act.

It could be any stimuli around your environment, a memory, a happening, or anything that would move you to act! Being on the brink of failure could be a motivator (Appendix C).

Motivation is what keeps you going.

Motivation is what gets you there to show what ya got!

Inspiration is the first step, and motivation the second.

You may have the motivation, but you'll eventually lose your motivation if you don't know why you're doing something. Likewise, you may have the inspiration, but you'll eventually quit if you don't have enough motivation to keep going.

Your thoughts, words, and deeds can both inspire and motivate you and others.

Motivation is what gets you out of bed in the
morning and keeps you up at night.

Motivation is the most powerful and least expensive cosmetic on the market. It's your motivation that attracts the people and resources needed to achieve your goals. Most people want to be around someone who is up to something, excited, and driven to accomplish something important.

What Motivates All Human Behavior?

We act for one of two reasons, either to avoid pain and or to gain pleasure.

- **What Pleasures do humans seek?** Love, recognition, happiness, power, encouragement, reward, success, food, meaningful work, comfort, promotions, freedom, convenience, free time, money, health, and anything else that could keep them in their Comfort Zone (Chapter 13).

- **What Pain do humans avoid?** Failure, boring and repetitive work, do-overs, loss, embarrassment, mistakes, frustration, setbacks, waiting on others, wasting time, indecision, "unacceptable" behavior, conflict, struggle, uncertainty, physical or mental discomfort, fear, or anything that could take them out of their Comfort Zone.

What's Inspiration?

Inspiration is the igniter, and Motivation is the driver!

Inspiration is the power to stimulate the intellect or emotions through an external source like:

- **Feeling:** Something you emotionally experienced (war, cancer, bankruptcy, divorce, or an accident).

- **Sight:** Something you saw or read (child, animal, movie, picture, TV, device, book, article, or letter).

- **Hearing:** Something someone said (speech or kind word) or by music (song, hymn, or a marching band).

- **Smell:** Something you smell that reminds you of something good or bad.

- **Touch:** Someone who touches you in a way that reminds you of something good or bad.

What's Intrinsic Motivation?

From studies involving more than 6,000 people, *Professor* **Steven Reiss** proposed a theory that finds these 16 basic desires that motivate human behavior:

- Acceptance: The need for approval.
- Curiosity: The need to learn.
- Eating: The need for food.
- Family: The need to raise children.
- Honor: The need to be loyal to traditional values.
- Idealism: The need for social justice.
- Independence: The need for individuality.
- Order: The need to be organized, stable, and predictable.
- Physical activity: The need for exercise.
- Power: The need for influence of will.
- Romance: The need for sex.
- Saving: The need to collect.
- Social contact: The need for relationships.
- Status: The need for social standing and importance.
- Tranquility: The need to be safe.
- Vengeance: The need to strike back.

What's Extrinsic Motivation?

Extrinsic motivators are external motivators and include positive motivators (like money, recognition, praise, awards, medals, trophies, or a crowd cheering during competition) and negative motivators (like coercion or the threat of punishment). **Abraham Maslow's** Theory of motivation is one of the most widely discussed theories of motivation and essentially states that humans have wants and desires which influence behavior.

> *Only unsatisfied needs influence behavior.*
> *Satisfied needs don't.*

Since your needs are many, they are arranged in order of importance, from the basic to the complex. You can advance to the next level of needs only after the lower-level needs are at least minimally satisfied. The further you progress up the hierarchy, the more individuality, humanness, and psychological health you'll experience.

Here are Maslow's motivations, from highest to lowest:

- Self-actualization: Achieving your true potential, including creative activities.

- Esteem needs: Self-esteem, Recognition, and Achievement.

- Belongingness needs: Love, Relationships, and Friends.

- Safety Needs: Safety, Security, Shelter, and Health.

- Basic or Physiological needs: Hunger, Thirst, Warmth, and Sleep.

Here's an example of Maslow's Motivations:

This page is intentionally left blank.

2
BY STRIVING FOR
SERENITY

"Mere mortals have talents and flaws. Successful ones know how to use their talents. But happy ones have learned to accept their flaws."
- John Lithgow, 3d Rock from the Sun.

How does *Serenity* affect your *Awareness?*

Serenity is that quality of utter calm and unruffled repose of quietude or tranquility.

No discussion of awareness will make any sense until you understand the difference between what you can and cannot control.

This simple prayer, which I learned during my recovery from alcoholism, helped me finally answer this life-altering question:

What are the only things in life I can control and therefore change?

THE SERENITY PRAYER

"God, grant me the <u>Serenity</u> *to*

<u>Accept</u> *the things I cannot change,*

<u>Courage</u> *to change the things I can,*

and the <u>Wisdom</u> *to know the difference*

- Reinhold Niebuhr

And these answers changed my life forever.

**In this life,
You cannot control or change other people, places,
things, situations, or circumstances.**

**The only things you can control and therefore change
are your thoughts, words, and deeds.**

And all those years, I thought I could control and change other people. What a waste of time and energy. This may come as a shocking epiphany for many of you because you've probably made the same mistake.

Yes, you can influence them, but you can't control or change them. You can only control and therefore change yourself.

This concept is crucial because until you learn to truly control what you can control (your thoughts, words, and deeds), you'll never influence anyone to help you consistently produce excellent results.

This happens because you sometimes confuse the word *control* with *responsibility*. You think they're the same, and they're not! Yes, you may be responsible for your family and your team members. However, you don't control them and can't change them. You can only influence them. And you can only do so after you've controlled or changed your thoughts, words, and deeds. But thanks to their free agency, they control and can change themselves (some don't know it yet).

Serenity affects your values, beliefs, lifestyle, work, family, and friends. It's also the absence of fussing, fuming, fighting, worrying, and blaming. Whichever definition you choose, Serenity brings you that feeling of wellness, peace, and harmony with your environment.

Before continuing, let's review the most important terms that define Serenity: Courage, Acceptance, and Wisdom.

What does Courage have to do with Serenity?

To truly change your life means being willing to initiate new behaviors and step outside your Comfort Zone (Chapter 13). This transformation is a scary process. That's why it takes courage. Both fear and courage are learned through your interactions with family and friends throughout life.

Some parents allow greater freedom for growth than others. Some neighborhoods and cultures expect greater courage than others. You have your history from which to draw upon, but you can purposefully move forward on your own. If you never attempted to move out of your Comfort Zone, you'd still be lying in your crib, unable to walk. When you develop a stream of small successes where you feel safe, you're encouraged to try even more.

Count your small victories and move along the path you've chosen with courage.

What does Acceptance have to do with Serenity?

Acceptance is the act of mentally disengaging, releasing, or letting go of your *anchors-of-the-past* that prevent you from achieving happiness and success. It doesn't mean forgetting. Acceptance is also about being open to new ideas, setting aside judgments, and feeling free to explore and make new choices.

You're now free to make better choices. You can choose more attainable and winnable options, especially when it comes to those battles you fight every day within yourself. If you're searching for serenity and peace in your life, acceptance is critical. There's great wisdom in these ten simple sentences (above), but only if you apply them to your life. Acceptance is about being accountable to yourself. Here, you've learned from your past mistakes, so you're now free to move forward. You can only control, change, and conquer yourself.

Reaching Acceptance and Peace

Our lives are God's gift to us, what we do with them is our gift to God.
When it's time to die, make sure that's all you have to do.
Nothing can be accomplished until we take the first step.
None are so poor as those whose only wealth is money.
Do what you can where you are with what you have.
Showers of blessings come from storms of adversity.
The time to make friends is before you need them.
Leaders who serve will serve as good leaders.
Worry ends where faith begins.
Time – use it or lose it.
- Carmen Stine

Why do you need Wisdom to achieve Serenity?

Wisdom is needed to discern the difference between what you can and can't control. Furthermore, true wisdom comes when you realize that all the control you'll ever need to achieve true happiness and fulfillment is already yours. Wisdom lets you know that you have choices. You can choose to change. You can choose where to concentrate your time and energy. You can decide what's important today and take the appropriate action. Without the wisdom to know the difference between what you can and can't change, you'll easily become overwhelmed and will unknowingly surrender your serenity.

How can you achieve True and Lasting Serenity?

True serenity is a calmness of mind: a state free from agitation of the mind, spirit, disturbance, or turmoil. True serenity can only be achieved through the timeless and conscious process of wisely choosing where to focus your spiritual, mental, and physical energy. Working toward serenity is an ongoing process for us all.

Serenity, like perfection, isn't attainable, but if you keep striving for it, you'll achieve Peace of Mind.

You can choose to be part of the solution by thinking better thoughts, speaking better words, and taking better actions. Or you can choose to be part of the problem by blaming, gossiping, resenting, and hating. The latter provokes negative responses and leads to nowhere.

Nothing will get better until you decide to make yourself better. Unless you have sufficient awareness to understand which you can and can't control, you won't influence anyone. Learn to exercise control over yourself first. Once this is achieved, you're now ready to influence others. Don't confuse influence with manipulation. People instinctively know when they're being manipulated, and they'll resent you for it. Manipulation means that people are doing something for your reasons.

This knowledge is so powerful because it's simple, basic, and universally true, and useful. This guide is designed to expose you to the small and simple things that will help you magnify your natural abilities. Until then, you'll be fussing and fighting over what you can't change when you could be focusing your time and energy on changing that you can control. But how can you control and therefore change your attitude and behavior?

3
BY ADJUSTING
ATTITUDES AND BEHAVIORS

"People may hear your words, but they feel your attitude."
- John C. Maxwell

Attitude is feelings, beliefs, or opinions that you can choose, change, or ignore. Behavior is an action or reaction that responds to internal or external stimuli and usually reflects your beliefs and attitudes.

Your attitude is your point of view of approval or disapproval towards something that is either inborn or learned through experience that prepares you to respond or react in a pre-determined way.

You have the power to change your attitude and behavior anytime you choose.

What Attitudes do you Control?

Attitudes (your mood) come from your:

- Physical State (hormones, diet, pain, and illness).

- External Environment (learning from your parents and friends).

- Emotional State (anger, grief, resentment, pride, and fear).

Your attitudes create your:

- **Habits:** Habits are behaviors you repeat over and over again, many times unconsciously.

- **Perceptions:** Perceptions are the way you view something. You could be in a great mood (attitude) and suddenly encounter something that puts you in a bad mood.

- **Judgments:** Judgements are similar to perceptions, but judgments are more rigid, like things you believe are right or wrong.

The importance of your attitude cannot be overstated.

Attitude is everything.
It's more important than skill or reality.

Here are two of my favorite motivational speakers and writers over the years:

"Your attitude determines your altitude."
- Zig Zigler

Mr. Zigler was an American author, salesman, motivational speaker. And wrote over 30 books. His first book, *See You at the Top*, was rejected thirty-nine times before being published and is still in print today.

"When you expect the best, you release a magnetic force in your mind which by a law of attraction tends to bring the best to you."
- Norman Vincent Peale

Mr. Peale was an American minister and author who is best known for popularizing the concept of positive thinking, especially through his best-selling book *The Power of Positive Thinking*.

How do attitudes form?

Experience and Observation: Attitudes form from your experiences and may emerge from the personal experience of observing others.

Social Factors: Social roles and norms can strongly influence attitudes and dictate how people behave in certain situations.

Learning: What attitudes and beliefs have you inherited from your family about religion, politics, and sex that have influenced your behavior?

Conditioning: Consider how advertisers use classical conditioning to influence your attitude toward a particular product or service.

How can you change your attitude?

One great way to change your attitude is through subliminal affirmations and visualizations (Chapter 27). Attitudes are often the result of experience or upbringing, and they can have a powerful influence over behavior. While attitudes are enduring, they can be changed.

For example, what's your opinion on the death penalty? Chances are you have an opinion. You've developed attitudes about such issues, and these attitudes influence your beliefs as well as your behavior.

Tip: Next time you conduct a job interview, ask questions about their attitudes (how do you feel about (or what would you do in) this topic or situation? When was the last time this happened to you, and what did you do?)

What Behaviors do you Control?

What Words (Behaviors) do you control?

- **What you say:** Includes your choice of words, expressions, jokes, bad language, following-up, praise, recognition, relationships, feedback, asking, persuading, courtesy, and treating others with respect and kindness.

- **How you say it:** Includes your voice tonality, pause, inflection, intensity, volume, pronunciation, emotion, enthusiasm, and body language.

- **What you fail to say:** Includes withholding praise or recognition, corrections that you should have made, and not enforcing the standards. *These are often referred to as the Sins of Omission.*

What Deeds (Behaviors) do you control?

- **What you do:** Includes your habits, do's and don'ts, right vs. wrong, service, work ethic, abilities, effort, education, training, and personal mannerisms (manners, handshake, movement, posture, eye contact, dress, hygiene, grooming, gestures, energy, and enthusiasm).

- **How you do it:** Includes your attitude.

- **What you fail to do:** Includes your failure to perform your duty, catch mistakes, errors, and defects, act when it was your duty to do so, accept the consequences of your behavior, make corrections, offer appreciation and recognition, and meet standards. These are often referred to as *Sins of Omission.*

Note: Realize that you control all your behaviors and attitudes and can change them at any time. The most important thing you control is how you treat others - even when they treat you badly.

How about the behaviors and attitudes of others?

You already know that you have no control over other people, including their behaviors and attitudes.

However, you can mandate the behavior of others by using laws, ordinances, rules, and a code of conduct at work. Advertisers and social media change buyer behaviors every day.

Attitudes are much harder to change unless you can convince someone that the change is in their best interest.

My best advice, change your attitude first before attempting to influence the attitude of others. Then, by your example and gentle persuasion, begin the process of influencing the attitude of others by treating them with respect and kindness.

4
BY DEMONSTRATING
APPRECIATION

"Correction does much, but encouragement does more."
- Goethe

Effective people know they need positive and negative motivators in every company because there're consequences for your actions or inactions; sometimes good, sometimes not so good. *Positive Motivators* include both appreciation and recognition.

The purpose of Positive Motivators is to create

or reinforce desired performance.

What's the difference between Appreciation and Recognition?

- **Appreciation** is a *long-term strategy* that involves continuous steps that help build a strong foundation where members feel valued, respected, and supported. It's about supporting your members, not for what they do but for who they are (Chapter 4).

- **Recognition** is a *short-term celebration* provided AFTER achieving a specific result. Recognition is a great way to show members that you notice their excellent performance (Chapter 5).

The reality is that appreciation includes recognition, but in most cases, both terms are used interchangeably.

Which is better, appreciation or recognition?

A recent UC Berkley study revealed that:

- 23% of people who feel **'recognized'** are more effective and productive.

- 43% of people who feel **'appreciated'** are more effective and productive.

This means that members experience a 20% lift in their perception of their effectiveness and productivity from being *appreciated* rather than just *recognized*. Appreciation includes recognition, but in most cases, both terms are used interchangeably. It also means that:

Members who feel appreciated are more productive than those who don't feel that way.

And more importantly, ensure that appreciation is personalized for each member, rather than the old *"one size fits all."* The *bottom-line* is that the recipe for member satisfaction is a combination of both recognition and appreciation. It doesn't matter what you call it; the only thing that matters is what you do and how you do it.

By demonstrating Appreciation

The first type of *Positive Motivation* is *Appreciation*.

Appreciation is a long-term strategy that involves continuous steps that help build a strong foundation where members feel valued, respected, and supported not for what they do but for who they are.

Showing appreciation means praising, commending, complimenting, admiring, celebrating, endorsing, and contributing to their *Emotional Bank Account.*

An *Emotional Bank Account,* a concept developed by **Dr. Steven R. Covey** in his book, *The 7-Habits of Highly Effective People*, is a shorthand way of explaining a very complex series of human emotions by using a metaphor called the *Emotional Bank Account.*

Every time you treat someone with respect or kindness, you have just deposited into their *Emotional Bank Account.* For example, if you say *thank you* to someone privately, you could earn a $1.00 deposit into their account. However, saying *thank you* in front of everyone in your unit could be a $10.00 deposit.

And just the opposite behavior would result in a withdrawal. What does the bank balance look like for the members who work closely with you? This is an important question because it speaks to their motivation to serve and support you.

5

BY
RECOGNIZING
EXCELLENCE

"Don't worry when you are not recognized,
but strive to be worthy of recognition."
- Abraham Lincoln

The second type of *Positive Motivation* is *Recognition*.

Recognition is a short-term celebration AFTER
a member has demonstrated excellent performance
(achievement, service, or ability).

It's a great way to show members that you noticed their excellent performance and includes informal and formal recognition.

Informal Recognition

Many people think recognition must include trophies, plaques, or cash. This is untrue! The best recognition programs cost very little.

Here are a few things you can do to provide informal recognition.

1. By sending personal notes.

One of the most powerful motivational techniques is the power of the simple personal note. I still have the personal notes I received over the years from those I deemed effective. They took the time to sit down and write a note recognizing me for something small.

For two decades, **Jack Welch**, the former Chairman and CEO of *General Electric*, was famous for his simple personal notes to members. These notes through the years have become prized trophies to their recipients.

Take time to recognize members several levels below you by sending them a simple personal note. You've no idea how much this will mean to the receiver. If you recognize just one person every day or every week, the effect on your members will be immeasurable.

For maximum effect, put your favorite quote at the bottom and use a wide-tipped black pen on nice 6 X 9-inch personalized stationery, *"From the desk of..."*

Everyone likes to be noticed and recognized, especially in writing from the boss. So whom will you recognize tomorrow? Every week, on Wednesday and Friday, reach out and recognize someone for doing good. It could be a visit, a phone call, an email, or a personal note. Just do it!

2. By publicizing the recognition.

Recognize their success on the intranet, bulletin board, social pages, website, and blog post. Post pictures on social media so they can be publicly recognized. Share their successes more widely and demonstrate how you value your team members.

3. By seeking nominations from team members.

Managers can't be everywhere and don't often have an opportunity to notice good work as it happens. Ask team members to nominate members who have stepped up and done good work. Peer recognition validates and strengthens the bonds within the team.

4. By recognizing career milestones and personal achievements.

Career milestones include a work anniversary, a big sale, or earning a certification or license.

5. By rewarding members for proactive behavior.

Encourage behavior where members look for and anticipate problems and mistakes by checking, testing, inspecting, tracking, following up, and following through. Your objective here is to help them create the habit of anticipating problems. This way, you're preparing them to resolve problems before they become a crisis.

Proactive behavior means to prepare for, intervene in, or manage a situation, especially a negative or difficult one.

Here you're trying to resolve tomorrow's potential problems in advance.

Formal recognition normally includes cash awards, promotions, trips, plaques, bonuses, pay raises, and similar incentives. However, it's more about HOW you do it rather than what you do.

Formal recognition is normally given AFTER a member's performance has:

- Exceeded the desired performance level.

- Maintained their desired performance for at least a year.

- Enhanced their Professional Development (education, *training, or certification).

- Made significant improvements or other contributions.

I won't be addressing compensation or benefits here, except that if you intend to attract and retain the *best and the brightest,* compensation and benefits better be at least *on par* with the industry standard.

There are no ordinary people.

Everyone is extraordinary at something.

Your job is to find it!

Note: Doing your job or meeting your goals is expected performance and is always deserving of appreciation. However, it doesn't call for recognition unless the performance has been maintained for at least a year.

Do you have a Rewards Program?

Reward programs work if they're strongly linked to business objectives and members know what's expected of them. Members need to see the connection between their work and the overall goals of the company.

What are the different types of Rewards?

The different types of rewards include bonuses, variable pay, or stock options. In addition, structured programs can include regular recognition events such as banquets or breakfasts, member of the month or year recognition, or an annual report or yearbook that features members' accomplishments.

*To learn more about *Training*, available at **Amazon.com,** see page 5.

A job well done can also be recognized by providing additional support or empowering members with greater options of assignments to choose from and increased authority and autonomy.

Note: Recognition by itself may have a monetary value (such as a luncheon, gift certificates, or plaques), but money normally isn't given to recognize performance.

By recognizing someone in front of everyone.

Here's a great story:

> *"Years ago, **A. L. Williams**, an insurance company, used public award presentations to inspire and motivate their people to continuously surpass their goals. Every month, the company would gather all their people locally and hand out awards. The recognition of member and team performance, given in front of their peers, was the driving force that motivated others to exceed their **last-personal-best** performance. They tried harder to be more productive with their time, seeking ways to consistently produce excellent results, and become more effective, efficient, and consistent.*
>
> *The real motivation wasn't the award. It was the recognition for their time and effort presented publicly in front of their peers.*
>
> *Interestingly, those who continuously didn't receive recognition, although they tried hard, moved on to other companies or found something else to do more productive. So no one had to be fired."*

Effective people are in the business of unleashing human potential. As such, they find and bring out what makes each team member special. They know that praising someone, especially in front of their family, friends, and coworkers, is the most motivational thing they can ever do.

6

BY DEFINING ACCEPTABLE PERFORMANCE

"A coach is someone who can give correction
without causing resentment."
- John Wooden

When unacceptable performance (either results or behavior) is identified, you have two kinds of negative motivators you can use: correcting and punishing.

- **Correcting** is used for minor deviations from the desired performance (behavior or results). Correcting isn't punishment; it's part of the normal course of doing business and includes verbal corrections and rework Chapter 8).

- **Punishing** is used for more serious deviations from the desired performance or when corrective measures have proven unsuccessful, including reprimands, retraining, probation, termination, and even legal action (Chapter 9).

There are consequences to your actions (or inactions), sometimes good, sometimes not so good. Just know that the day will come when you need to use punishment to get someone's attention or correct unacceptable performance.

Important Definitions and Terms

Before we continue, let's define a few key terms:

- **Performance:** Performance includes both behavior and results.

- **Unacceptable:** Instead of using the term "bad" performance, let's change it to "unacceptable" performance. When trying to correct someone's "bad" performance, they often translate this to mean that they're a "bad" person that could cause them to become defensive. Doing so also defuses any potential conflict and helps the member make the correction.

- **Offense:** This is the specific result or behavior that was unacceptable.

What's Unacceptable Behavior

My definition of "unacceptable" behavior comes from the overall impact on the team and its effectiveness. Any definition of "unacceptable" behavior depends on the context.

However, you need a reliable standard for assessing if a member's behavior is acceptable or not, which you can then apply to any situation. Since teams do almost all work, any behavior that disrupts the team's stability, harmony, or productivity or the working environment is by definition "unacceptable."

Unacceptable behavior is any behavior that disrupts the stability, harmony, or productivity of the team or the work environment.

This means that any behavior that violates this standard is "unacceptable." Unacceptable behavior has a tangible impact on profitability. For example, missed objectives, declining productivity, increased sick days, higher turnover, and the time and money lost in hiring and training new members all diminish your profitability.

Here are the most common unacceptable behaviors:

- **Disrespectful behavior:** Disrespectful behaviors range from overt acts of abuse and "unacceptable" behavior to insidious actions so embedded in the culture that they seem normal, like gossip.

Disrespectful behavior is any behavior that creates a negative or threatening atmosphere in the workplace.

Examples include public humiliation, criticizing, interrupting, ridiculing, dismissing achievements, shouting, blaming, degrading a team member in front of others, inappropriate sarcasm, and speaking in a condescending or belittling way.

- **Disruptive Behavior:** Egregious conduct evident in the behavior or speech, like angry or rude outbursts, verbal or written threats and swearing, pushing or throwing objects, bullying, and threats or infliction of physical force.

- **Demeaning Behavior:** Patterns of debasing behavior that exploit the weakness of another, like:
  - ✓ Shaming, humiliation, demeaning comments, spiteful behavior, backstabbing behavior.
  - ✓ Nitpicking or faultfinding.
  - ✓ Censuring members in front of others.
  - ✓ Insults and insensitive jokes or remarks.
  - ✓ Sexual harassment and sexual innuendos.

- **Intimidating Behavior:** Behaviors or threats used by one member to control another, like:
  - ✓ Abuse of power through threats, coercion, and force of personality.
  - ✓ Overbearing, arrogant, patronizing behavior.
  - ✓ Sarcasm or taunting, and hostile notes or emails.
  - ✓ Invading another person's personal space intentionally.
  - ✓ Unjust verbal statements by someone in authority that result in distressful consequences for the recipient and others.

- **Dismissive Behavior:** Behavior that makes a member feel unimportant or uninformed, like:
  - ✓ Condescending or patronizing comments.
  - ✓ Gossiping.
  - ✓ Aloof, disinterested, or ignoring.
  - ✓ Slights due to gender or race.
  - ✓ Impatience.
  - ✓ Resistance to work collaboratively.
  - ✓ Refusal to value, recognize, acknowledge, or praise others.
  - ✓ Exclusionary and over-ruling behavior.

- **Passive-Aggressive Behavior:** On the surface, *Passive-Aggressive (or PA) Behavior* may appear as stubbornness or a polite unwillingness to agree. However, the PA person is trying to manipulate you to turn to their way of thinking (or hope you'll give the work to someone else).

Passive-Aggressive (PA) Behavior describes someone who exhibits manipulative behavior within their personality.

The PA person, who could also be your boss, may use these techniques as a form of intimidation. They'll sulk when you ask for their help or may simply take an undue amount of time to decide. This is their way of showing displeasure by using passive-aggressive behavior.

Unacceptable behavior is never someone else's fault!

The PA person hopes that you won't ask them to do anything anymore by exhibiting this behavior. They hope that their behavior will be too off-putting and that next time, you'll ignore them or offer some special concession to get them to do their job. Don't fall for it!

PA behavior includes, but is not limited to:

- ✓ Selective disobedience, contentious behavior, delaying, failing to return and report, resisting, and *blowing it off.*
- ✓ Dissension, murmuring, arguing after the decision is made, undermining, and rebelling.
- ✓ Sarcasm, mockery, pushing back, belaboring, and not participating.
- ✓ Any outward display of displeasure or nonsupport.
- ✓ Chronic lateness to meetings and sluggish response to requests.

- **Negative body language:** Subtle, unspoken behavior that may seem innocent enough but is nonetheless disrespectful, including:

  - ✓ Staring or glaring, sighing, making gestures, and pointing.

  - ✓ Making faces, raising eyebrows, and rolling eyes.

  - ✓ Positioning their body to exclude others.

- **Rude behaviors:** Rude behavior includes:
  - ✓ Checking your phone constantly, being late, and interrupting.
  - ✓ Grooming in public (flossing, scratching, picking your nose, combing hair, applying makeup, or cutting nails).
  - ✓ Burping and coughing without covering your mouth.
  - ✓ Keeping others waiting, littering, and talking over someone.

What're Unacceptable Results?

All companies produce a product, service, or both.

Unacceptable results mean that a product or service failed to meet the established standard or the customer's expectations.

This means that any result that violates this standard is "unacceptable."

For an Unacceptable Service:

An unacceptable service is normally identified by a customer and results in either a new service for free, their money back, or both. The most common cause of an unacceptable service includes a failure to produce the advertised result, problems with the service providers, failure to arrive on time, and a price increase.

For an Unacceptable Product:

An unacceptable product is normally identified by a Quality Control process that inspects products before leaving your unit. If not, the customer should receive a new product for free, their money back, or both. The most common causes of an unacceptable product include a failure to perform as advertised, damage during shipping, missing items, price increased, broke during use.

How can you enhance the quality of your results?

Quality is a result of effectiveness, efficiency, and consistency.

What's Effectiveness?

This refers to the output produced from your business systems.

**Effectiveness means successfully producing
a desired or intended result.**

Effectiveness is future-oriented and involves achieving goals, anticipating change, and striving for innovation.

Effectiveness First, then Efficiency!

What's Efficiency?

Once you're effective, look for ways to become more efficient. This is done by finding ways to make your products and services better (faster, easier, lighter, smaller, more innovative, safer, and more secure)?

**Efficiency means taking something that's
working well and making it better.**

Your job is to make things better than you found them. Establish a reputation as the one who gets things done and is effective, efficient, and consistently produces excellent results. Efficiency focuses on the present and involves process improvement.

What's Consistency?

Consistency is critical to achieving success over time. For example, would you buy a car from a company that only produced a quality product, only one out of one hundred cars?

**Consistency means maintaining a standard or
repeating a task with minimal variation.**

What happens to inconsistent NFL Football Coaches near the end of the season? They get fired! It's not personal; it's business! Consistency is fundamental to excellence, even if the output is consistently bad. You can improve any system if it's consistent in its output.

Quality Results =

Effectiveness + Efficiency + Consistency.

7
BY DOING THE
RIGHT THING

"Stay focused on your mission, remain steadfast in your pursuit of excellence, and always do the right thing."
- Mark Esper

What's the *Right Thing?* Do you always do what's right or what's easiest? Here are several useful definitions to help you demonstrate the *Right Thing:*

What did you learn in Kindergarten?

From the book, *All I really need to know, I learned in Kindergarten,* by **Robert Fulghum,** you'll find a great list of desired behavior to help you do the right thing.

"These are the (eleven of the sixteen) things I learned:

- Share everything.
- Play fair.
- Don't hit people.
- Put things back where you found them.
- Clean up your own mess.
- Don't take things that aren't yours.
- Say you're sorry when you hurt somebody.
- Wash your hands before you eat.
- Flush.
- Live a balanced life - learn some, think some, draw, paint, sing, dance, play, and work every day some.
- When you go out in the world, watch out for traffic, hold hands and stick together.

Everything you need to know about life is in these twelve things somewhere.

What's the Golden Rule?

Character includes *The Golden Rule*, love, basic sanitation, ecology, politics, equality, and sane living. Character doesn't happen automatically and is too important to be left to chance.

Your effectiveness depends on it. And there is such a thing as *Right* and *Wrong* behavior.

We all have a duty to teach others, especially the young, that honesty is superior to lying, fairness to cheating and stealing, and caring to indifference.

What do some Religions say about Right and Wrong Behavior?

The ultimate guide for *Right* behavior is the *Golden Rule*, and here's what some religions consider their *Golden Rule*.

- **Christianity:** *"As ye would that men should do to you, do ye also to them likewise."*

- **Islam:** *"No one of you is a believer until he desires for his brother that which he desires for himself."*

- **Hinduism:** *"One should never do that to another which one regards as injurious to one's own self."*

All religions teach their members the same thing;
to treat others as they wish to be treated –
with respect and kindness.

What did you learn from your parents?

From an early age, I learned these simple lessons about accountability or doing the *Right Thing*:

- If you lose, damage, or break something that doesn't belong to you, you need to fix it or buy it.

- If you borrow something, you need to return it in the same or better condition than you found it.

- If you back into and damage someone's car, and they're not around, you need to leave your name and number.

- If you were mean or disrespectful to someone, you need to apologize (Chapter 19).

So, what's *Right* behavior? It all starts by treating everyone with respect and kindness!

8
BY CORRECTING
UNACCEPTABLE PERFORMANCE

"Correction does much, but encouragement does more."
- Goethe

What do you do when a team member's performance is unacceptable? When this happens, you have two kinds of negative motivators you can use: correcting and punishing.

By taking these steps BEFORE an offense

Step 1. Know the Standards of Excellence.

Before making any correction, you need to know all the company's written, implied, and expected standards, especially if a union is involved. In addition, behavioral standards are normally provided to all team members as part of In-Processing and available in writing as part of the company's *Code of Ethics* and other compliance documents.

Step 2. Find what needs to be corrected.

When you notice something that needs to be corrected, immediately and discreetly speak with the member to ensure the correction is made. Never walk by something that needs to be corrected, or you'll be sending the message that it's not important. When correcting, you're training members on what's acceptable and what's not.

Step 4. Make it Private!

This is the most important step before you can successfully correct anyone. Either do so quietly or move to somewhere where you won't be interrupted. This is the best way to show respect.

Step 3. Choose your words carefully.

When a member fails to meet a standard, this is called an "offense." If you're trying to correct someone's "bad" behavior, they often hear this to mean that they're a "bad" person that could cause them to become defensive. To avoid this, instead of using the term "bad," use the term "unacceptable." The assumption here is that their behavior or results are something the member can correct.

Step 5. Separate the member from the offense.

When you separate the offense from the member, you're now ready to discuss the offense. By doing so and focusing on their "behavior or results," will defuse any potential conflict and help the member make the correction.

Never attempt to correct someone's "attitude."

Focus on their behavior instead.

If your focus is on the member rather than the offense, you'll create an adversarial relationship.

Step 6. Set clear boundaries.

Appropriate boundaries are an important part of any healthy relationship. Let the member know what's acceptable and what's not. Establish clear consequences if they fail to respect your boundaries (Chapter 9). A good example is unacceptable language and jokes.

Step 7. Know how to deal with excuses.

What's the difference between a *Reason* and an *Excuse* (Appendix G)?

Here's a simple rule:

Reasons are believable, understandable, and forgivable.

Excuses aren't.

By taking these steps AFTER an offense.

How do you make corrections? Here are the most important steps to take:

Step 1. Give the member a chance to respond.

Give the member a chance to speak without interrupting. Let them know that you hear and respect what he has to say. Try rephrasing what he said to ensure you understand him correctly. Show that you're listening actively by nodding, making eye contact, and using phrases like *"Okay," "Right,"* or *"I hear you."*

Step 2. Hold the member accountable for his performance.

No discussion of correcting someone's performance can occur without a firm understanding of *accountability,* which isn't something you're born with. It comes as you mature and become a *Fully Functioning Adult.*

Unfortunately, very few people in the workplace will have a fully developed sense of *accountability or maturity.* If they did, your job would be easy (Appendix G).

Accountability means no excuses, no complaining, no blaming, and no deception!

The day you fully accept that you're entirely *accountable* for your success or failure and realize that no one is coming to your rescue will be the first day of your peak performance. And there's very little you can't be, do, or have after you accept this motto:

"If it is to be, it is up to me!" – Anonymous.

Step 3. Use these eight steps from the Correcting Process:

The Correcting Process	
1. Private	Find somewhere private to discuss the potential offense.
2. Observation	*"I noticed, saw, heard, or have been told."*
3. Verify	*"Is this true and why did it happen?*
Continue only if the offense is true and the member's reason was invalid.	
4. Effect	Explain how this offense makes you feel. *"I feel, think, believe, or I'm concerned that..."*
5. Request	State what you want the member to do to correct the offense. *"I need you to.... (Start, stop, or change)."*
6. Consequences	*"Bob, if this behavior happens again, it will be dealt with more seriously."*
7. Expectation	*"You're one of my best team members. But I need you to fix this today."*
8. Commitment	*"How can you ensure me this won't happen again?"*

Notice that each step of the process has a suggested sentence to get you started. If the correcting process doesn't work, you may have to consider punishment (Chapter 9).

Here's an example of how *The Correcting Process* can be used.

> *You overhear one of your Direct Reports, Bob, screaming at one of his team members. Bob was very upset over something. You interrupt and ask Bob to walk with you to a vacant room.*
>
> *You close the door and say, "Bob, I noticed you were screaming at Sally about something. I'm concerned because this isn't acceptable behavior, but more importantly, this isn't you.*
>
> *I need you to calm down, apologize to Sally, and refrain from screaming at anyone. Okay?" Pause: "Bob, I'm surprised at this behavior. I expect much better from you. You're one of my people. But I need you to fix this today."*

In this example, you used *The Correcting Process* to guide your actions. And you can ask for an explanation. But what does it matter?

His behavior was unacceptable. Your actions were immediate, appropriate, private, and direct. You might also recommend that he take some time off.

9
BY PUNISHING
UNACCEPTABLE PERFORMANCE

"We need to understand the difference between discipline and punishment. Punishment is what you do to someone; discipline is what you do for someone."
- Zig Ziglar

The second type of negative motivator is to administer punishment. Punishment is considered for serious offenses or when previous attempts to correct a member's performance have been unsuccessful. No discussion of punishment will make any sense unless you understand the concept of Justice and Mercy.

To Apply Justice (assuming the person works for you), ask:

- Did the member do something wrong?

- Why did they do it or fail to do it?

- What damage occurred?

To Apply Mercy (assuming this person did something wrong or unacceptable), ask:

- Did he know he was doing something unacceptable?

- Did he accept accountability for his actions or inactions?

- Is this a repeat offense? If so, the punishment is increased.

You can also suspend the punishment for a specific time. Don't forget to discuss the situation with your boss and Human Resources before taking action.

What are the questions to ask before administering punishment?

- Is the punishment Fair and Reasonable?
- Is it Progressive (verbal reprimand, written reprimand)?
- Is it Equitable (the same offense receives the same punishment)?
- Do you have the authority, or do you need your boss?
- Are your boss and HR in agreement?

What are your options for punishment?

Examples include a written reprimand, retraining, probation, transfer to another unit, loss of income, demotion, privilege or access, poor performance review, termination, and legal action. There are consequences to your actions (or inactions), sometimes good, sometimes not so good. Just know that the day will come when you'll need to use punishment to get someone's attention.

What if you need to let someone go?

During your time in the workforce, you'll be faced with the situation of having to let someone go. It's inevitable. All 50 US States (except Montana) have an *"at-will"* clause in their employment contracts. This means that your boss can let you go at any time, without reason.

The Peter Principle is a concept in management theory formulated by **Laurence J. Peter**. The selection of a candidate for a position is based on the member's performance in their current role rather than their abilities relevant to the intended role. Thus, members stop being promoted once they can no longer perform effectively.

However, before you do so, answer these questions:

- Do you have the authority to let someone go?
- Have you done all you can do to save the person?
- Are your efforts to save the person documented?
- Have you kept your boss and HR appraised?

Remember, the day will come for everyone when your best won't be good enough. This doesn't mean that they're a bad person. It just means that the position wasn't a good fit. And wouldn't it be nice if you had a boss who helped you move on to where you would be more productive? Remember that when it's your turn to let someone go.

If you want to keep your team motivated, ensure you take immediate and decisive action with those who are a distraction to the team. If you don't, it will become a de-motivator.

10
BY KEEPING
THE PEACE

"Success isn't measured by money or power or social rank. Success is measured by your discipline and inner peace."
- Mike Ditka

Have you ever worked somewhere where there was at least one person who stood out as a troublemaker? You know - that one person who was always late to meetings, a chronic complainer, negative attitude, and caused drama, disharmony, and distractions? There seems to be one in every office. This behavior is unacceptable and can't be tolerated.

Keeping the Peace means helping others cope with the ebb and flow of their emotions.

If someone failed to learn how to play nice with the other kids in Kindergarten, do you really want him on your team? Think about what it's like to work in a Fire House. Firefighters work together for two reasons: to get the job done and not endanger their fellow Firefighters' lives.

This doesn't mean that everyone likes each other. However, it does mean that they separate their working relationships from their personal relationships. And, if they can't keep them separate and the unacceptable behavior spills over into their working environment, causing disharmony within the team, one or both should be released for the team's good.

I believe **Dorothy Thompson** had it right when she said,

"Peace is not the absence of conflict, but the ability to cope with it."

Conflict is inevitable and expected. Not all conflict is bad unless it becomes personal, abusive, or violent. Effective people respond quickly, privately, and treat everyone with respect and kindness. In the workplace, you're responsible for and accountable to your boss for everything that happens or fails to happen within your unit. You're also accountable to your boss for your team members' behavior and results (Appendix G).

Unacceptable behavior is never someone else's fault!

Here are a few suggestions on how to *Keep the Peace.*

Do you know the standards?

Know your organization's standards of behavior and consult with your boss and HR before taking any serious action. Unacceptable behavior or results is the enemy of teamwork and cannot be tolerated for any reason.

Is it your job to judge others?

If you're the boss, absolutely, but with limitations. It's not your place to judge or treat anyone as being a bad person. Focus instead on their behavior and results, not the person! That means no name-calling, labeling, or stereotyping. It's also unwise to judge someone's attitude; assess their behavior instead.

Behavior includes what they say and do, what they fail to say and do, and the consequences. For example, suppose someone smells bad (poor hygiene due to not bathing). This behavior is something someone failed to do, which is unacceptable behavior-especially if it causes disharmony within the team.

While it's your duty to judge the performance of those in your charge, it's not your duty to judge whether anyone is a good or bad person. Judging behavior is everyone's responsibility, although it's done infrequently. For example, if you see unacceptable behavior outside of work and don't want to confront the person, report it to someone in authority or dial 911 and let the Police sort it out.

What's conflict?

Workplace conflict is a state of discord caused by the actual or perceived opposition of needs, values, and interests between people working together. Conflict between members means a serious disagreement or argument. Conflict can also be a disagreement or argument among teams or members *characterized by antagonism and hostility. This type of conflict is usually fueled by a team member against another attempting to reach a different objective.

Conflict and contention are normal, natural, and expected, especially in the workplace. This happens because everyone is at a different level of maturity, a different level of accountability (Appendix G).

*To learn more about *Character*, available at **Amazon.com,** see page 5.

Conflict is inevitable because you can't please all the people all the time, no matter what you do. So, get used to it and prepare for it. Taking offense is a choice.

No one can hurt your feelings or offend you without your permission.

So, don't avoid difficult conversations. Preparation is the key to handling difficult conversations. Learn to use the *Correcting Process* (Chapter 8). The sooner you have the private conversation, the better. If it's serious or a repeat offense, document it using the process recommended by Human Resources and Company Policy.

Is conflict always destructive?

Conflict happens naturally. The clash of thoughts and ideas is a part of the human experience. It can be destructive if left unchecked. However, it's not always negative. It can also be a great way of generating more meaningful solutions to problems. Conflict can be an opportunity for learning and understanding the differences. These positive outcomes can be reached through effective conflict resolution. You can work in harmony despite conflict if you know how to manage these struggles.

This page is intentionally left blank.

11
BY RESOLVING
CONFLICT

"People like to say that the conflict is between good and evil.
The real conflict is between truth and lies."
- Don Miguel Ruiz

No one likes face-to-face confrontations. But you can't avoid them! But you don't have to be a jerk.

Conflict resolution is your ability to alleviate or eliminate the source of human conflict by using mediation, arbitration, coaching, dispute resolution, forgiveness, and active listening.

No one likes face-to-face confrontations. But you can't avoid them! But you don't have to be a jerk. However, it doesn't have to be adversarial if you know what you're doing.

Unacceptable behavior or results
should never be overlooked.

Other team members and your boss are watching and expecting you to consistently enforce the standards and hold members accountable for their unacceptable behavior and results. Generally, there are two different situations where conflict will occur: between two team members and between you and a team member.

Conflict between Team Members

As the boss, you're expected to be the *Peace Maker*. Arguments and disagreements can be good unless members talk over each other without listening, raise their voices, use unacceptable language, blame, make excuses, or are disrespectful. Here are the most important things to do when in this situation:

Step 1. Don't choose sides or get involved in the confrontation.

Remain objective and focus on their unacceptable behavior, not the person or their attitude. Don't get sucked into the dispute because you don't want your behavior to be called into question.

Step 2. Intervene and issue a Warning.

If the behavior of any member becomes unacceptable, warn them that their behavior is unacceptable, and if it continues, you will stop the meeting. If necessary, physically separate both members to return the environment to civility so work can resume.

Step 3. If it continues, end the meeting.

No one likes a hostile workplace. These distractions can only diminish your ability to consistently produce excellent results and can't be tolerated.

Step 4. If both parties cannot reconcile their differences.

As adults, if both members cannot reconcile their differences, one or both may need to be removed from the team. You are doing this to protect the *Health and Welfare* of your team (Chapter 38).

Conflict between you and a Team Member

Here are the most important things to consider when a team member treats you with disrespect. If someone treats you with disrespect, don't overreact! That's what the other member wants you to do.

If in a Group Setting:

Let's assume that you were in your team meeting when one of your team members said that one of your decisions was stupid. Disrespectful YES, but don't overreact. When appropriate, take a break (or wait until the meeting is over) and move to a more private, one-on-one setting by asking the member to walk with you.

If in a Private Setting:

Let's assume that you're in a private setting:

- Follow the steps from the *Correcting Process* (Chapter 8).
- Master the Art of Apologizing (Chapter 19).

12
BY DEMONSTRATING
MORAL COURAGE

"It is curious that physical courage should be so common
in the world and moral courage so rare."
- Mark Twain.

When it comes to moral courage, the fear of someone saying NO is a powerful emotional roadblock until you realize that they're not rejecting you as a person, just your request.

Moral courage is standing up for the truth, for what's right, for yourself, and for all those for whom you're responsible, even when you're the only one standing.

You may be asking the wrong person or asking the wrong question at the wrong time. This fear keeps you from asking for help from others. When in doubt, ask! Value yourself enough to get the answers you need to move forward.

Asking for help is a sign of strength, not a sign of weakness.

Not knowing you need help is a sign of ignorance.

Needing help and not asking for it is a sign of stupidity.

You can't control how others respond to you. However, you can control what you say and how you say it. Not everyone's going to say YES. Every NO isn't a personal rejection. An answer of NO is only a response to your presentation. It's also an indication of where the other person is coming from at the time you asked.

If you fail to go after what you want, you'll never have it.

If you're too afraid to ask, the answer will always be NO.

If you don't step forward, you'll always be where you are now.

Maybe the other person needs to be more informed to reach a YES. Also, since asking is a numbers game, every No response moves you closer to a YES, especially if you find out their reasons for saying NO.

Don't process an objection as a rejection. Objections are usually a request for more information. You have yet to give them a compelling enough reason to say YES. This is precisely why the best salespeople at the top of their profession finally close the sale (get a YES) only after receiving their fifth NO.

Asking is a numbers game.

Anyone in sales will tell you that,

"Some will, Some won't, So what, Next."

Keep going! Don't let rejection stop you!

Assess why people repeatedly say NO and modify your future presentations accordingly. Re-educate them as to the real value of your request. You have no control over other people, places, things, and situations. However, you can control your thoughts, words, and deeds.

What are the most important things you can do to demonstrate moral courage?

- By setting high standards and striving to maintain those standards.

- By making the tough decisions, the ones that make you unpopular (Appendix B).

- By having the courage to stand up for your members. Be their voice!

- By accepting the risk, regardless of the personal fallout.

- By doing the right thing rather than the easy or popular thing.

- By speaking up in meetings to praise members who do good work.

- By paying it forward, lifting others up, sponsoring them for life, and asking them to do the same.

By stopping the insanity of trying to be popular.

No matter what you do, you can't make someone like you. Some people will like you and others won't. You have no control over other people.

Being in-charge isn't a popularity contest.

No matter what you do, you can't please all the people all the time. You can only be respected by treating people with respect and kindness. And this is the best way to consistently produce excellent results.

Instead of trying to be popular, be yourself and treat everyone with respect and kindness. If anyone misunderstands your kindness as a weakness, speak with them privately and explain the difference. It's your job to enforce the standards, to *hold-the-line* when it comes to excellent performance.

If someone still has a problem, remind them that they can always work somewhere else if they're not happy. But you don't have to be an abusive jerk about it. This isn't being mean - it's being direct.

If you're doing your job right, someone will be upset with you. In most cases, they'll be upset because they've yet to fully mature and accept personal accountability for their actions and the consequences. If a member isn't meeting the standards, and you fail to tell him the truth, you're being disrespectful. It's your job to tell the truth, but with respect and kindness-behind closed doors.

Use the *Correcting Process* (Chapter 8). What they do next is up to them. You have no control over what they do. It's their job to correct their performance (results and behavior).

It takes moral courage to make corrections, maintain standards, assess performance, discipline, release members, and tell your boss what he doesn't want to hear, like the Truth.

Do you have the courage to rise to the occasion?

This page is intentionally left blank.

13
BY EXPANDING YOUR LEARNING ZONE

"The comfort zone is the great enemy to creativity; moving beyond it necessitates intuition, which in turn configures new perspectives and conquers fears."
- Dan Stevens

Do you know how to expand your learning zone to overcome the fear that has held you from achieving your true potential?

To better understand Fear, you must first understand your Comfort Zone. We all have a Comfort Zone, so that's no surprise. The surprise comes when you take a closer look at what really caused your Fear.

You might think that if you step outside your **Comfort Zone**, you'll be in your **Danger Zone**. After all, that's what you've learned over millions of years of evolution; it's called the *fight or flight response.*

There's great comfort in the familiar, simple, and predictable. We're all creatures of habit. But how do you gain experience if you stay in the familiar? How can you reach your true potential by staying in the familiar? Actually, you can't.

You'll never reach your true potential by in the familiar. You won't experience true joy by staying in your Comfort Zone.

Growth and excitement in life can only come from living outside your Comfort Zone, into the unknown, every second of your existence. But do you have to be in Danger to experience growth and excitement? No.

You have three zones: your Comfort, Learning, and Danger Zone.

Your **Comfort Zone** is where you feel safe and warm. This is the zone you are in when watching TV and seeing other people skydiving, wishing it could be you. Next is your **Learning Zone**. This is the zone you are in when you're learning, growing, stretching, and achieving. This is the zone you are in when you are skydiving, with certified and licensed instructors. Yes, you were nervously excited and scared but glad to be alive.

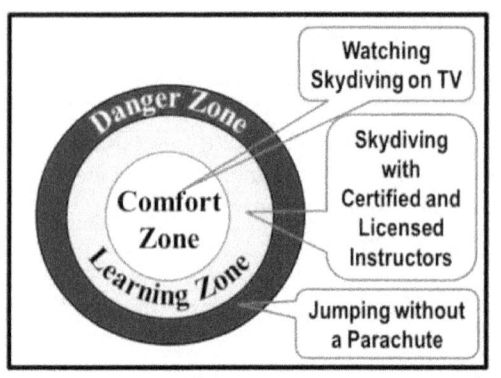

And the last outer layer is your **Danger Zone**. This is the zone where your life is truly in danger. This is the zone you would be in if you jumped out of an airplane without a parachute.

Unfortunately, your brain's been hard-wired to believe that your Danger Zone and your Learning Zone are the same, and they're not!

Your brain sends you the same Fear messages when you're in both your Danger or Learning Zone. This means that most, if not all, of the Fear messages you've received during your lifetime were when you were in your Learning Zone.

Your brain still sends you "danger messages" when you're only trying to learn new things, trying new ways of doing things, striving to achieve your goals, stepping forward with new ideas, and meeting new people.

Your fears have stopped you from growing
and living your life to its true potential – even
though you were in no real danger.

Being out of your Comfort Zone and into your Learning Zone is good for you. If you lived your life in your Learning Zone, every second of your existence, what an incredible life you'd have. Your Learning Zone is where you are when you are excited, growing, learning, achieving, reaching, stretching, struggling, and becoming better in the process.

Life begins where your Comfort Zone ends.

14
BY DEMONSTRATING ASSERTIVENESS

"Although individual temperaments vary, boys are designed to be more assertive, audacious, and excitable than girls are."
- James Dobson

Assertiveness is a critical life skill and can be learned and used as an effective mode of communication.

When you're assertive, you can:

- Express your views clearly without being aggressive or hostile.
- Stand up for your rights reasonably and clearly.
- Allow others to do the same without allowing them to dominate.

Assertiveness is the quality of being self-assured and confident without being aggressive.

A subtler element of assertiveness is the courage to express your feelings, even about difficult problems, in a way that's respectful and honest. Being assertive is respectfully asking for what you need in a way that's not too timid nor too bold.

What's the difference between passive, aggressive, and assertive behavior?

- **Passive Behavior** is acting passively, and it's likely that your needs, feelings, and wants will go unfulfilled.
- **Aggressive Behavior** is acting forcefully to express your needs and wants freely, but often without thought for the feelings of others, and sometimes in a loud or intimidating manner.
- **Assertive Behavior** is to express your needs, wants, and feelings in a more constructive way, allowing others to express theirs.

If you behave passively, it's likely that your needs, feelings, and wants will go unfulfilled. On the other hand, if you behave aggressively, it's unlikely that you'll participate in genuinely fulfilling relationships and involve genuine *communication and respect.

*To learn more about *Communicating*, available at **Amazon.com,** see page 5.

It's important to be assertive to meet and express your needs, respect and communicate with others effectively, and engage in more fulfilling relationships. If you behave passively or aggressively but would like to become more assertive, start identifying the thought patterns causing your non-assertive behavior and find more effective ways of overcoming them. Many people think that if they express their opinion that someone doesn't like, they'll get upset, or if you express your feelings and needs, you may be selfish and don't deserve to have your needs met. If this is you, you may have low self-esteem and might benefit from professional help.

What do assertive people say?

"Thanks, but..." Statements:

"Thanks, but I need some time to myself right now."

"No thanks. It's not a priority for me right now." It's not necessary to give a reason.

"Thanks for thinking of me, but I think I'll pass on this one."

"Thanks for keeping me in the loop, but I can't make it this time."

"Thank you for sharing, but I'd like to hear from other people in the group."

"I" Statements:

"I didn't appreciate ____ (what you did, your tone of voice)."

"I disagree with you. I see the situation this way."

"I feel offended by your remark."

"I prefer" Statements: In a preference statement, you simply express your preference about an issue. "I prefer to…

"Need" Statements:

"I need to sit somewhere else because the sun is in my eyes."

"Would you please not smoke in here because I'm allergic to the smoke."

It's important to be assertive to meet and express your needs, respect and communicate with others effectively, and engage in more fulfilling relationships.

15
BY ELIMINATING
TOLERATIONS

"Our daily tolerations become our choices by default.
We willingly accepted our present fate in life largely because
we never realized we no longer have to tolerate what we've
grown accustomed to accepting as the norm."
- Joyce Kuntz

The tolerations addressed here have nothing to do with accepting others regardless of their gender, race, religion, or sexual preference.

Tolerations are the bad or unpleasant things
you allow to exist, happen, or be done.

Examples include when someone next to you is smoking, you're a non-smoker, or when the sun is in your eyes, and you're sitting in a meeting.

Recognize that these tolerations are a choice and not something you must endure because you've no other option. Some tolerations may be beyond your control, but most aren't.

What're you tolerating today, and what
will it take for you to stop?

The major reason to deal with your tolerations is to reduce stress, become more assertive, enhance your confidence, and stop being a victim.

The first step is to recognize them and put them up-front and center-stage in your consciousness. Then, decide which ones you control (Chapter 2).

Stop complaining and do something about it.

How can you eliminate some of your tolerations?

You have the personal power to change your response to your tolerations and your assertiveness. Be assertive and speak up. For the tolerations you can't change, find a way to reframe them in a more positive light. Explore other alternatives until you find a way to re-categorize them as things you can either change or accept.

When is it time to U-HALT?

It's impossible to be effective when you're uncomfortable, hungry, angry, lonely, or tired. Do you control your comfort, hunger, anger, loneliness, or fatigue? In most cases, yes! And, in most cases, you can do something about it. If you change what you're thinking, saying, or doing, you can eliminate these conditions. However, in most cases, you just continue being miserable when your suffering is self-induced.

If you're angry, what's the source of your anger? Since anger is a secondary emotion caused by another emotion (like resentment), what's the primary cause of your anger? Deal with the cause by changing your thoughts or removing yourself from the situation. That's right; just walk away. The real trick here is to notice these conditions. If so, U-HALT and take the appropriate action to become centered once again. These actions are within your control.

Here's a great story:

One day I went to visit a friend. As we sat on his porch, reliving our youthful indiscretions, I noticed that his dog was yelping in pain every two minutes.

I asked my friend, What's wrong with your dog? His response was, "He's just lying on a nail." My response was, "Why doesn't he just lay somewhere else?" To this, my friend said, "Oh, I guess it doesn't hurt that bad."

Are you tolerating things in life because they just don't hurt that bad? This is also the classic definition of complacency.

16
BY DEMONSTRATING
EMPATHY

"A prerequisite to empathy is simply paying
attention to the person in pain."
- Daniel Goleman

Empathy enables you to feel their emotions and sincerely offer help and support.

Empathy is your capacity to understand another by being able to imagine yourself in their situation.

Your team members may share many details of their personal lives, or they might prefer to keep them more private. However, even if you don't know the details of their families and values, you can still have empathy and treat them like you understand their emotions.

There are two levels of empathy: Cognitive and Affective.

- **Cognitive empathy** means that you're capable of understanding other people's thoughts and feelings.

- **Affective empathy**, in addition to understanding, means that you're capable of feeling other people's emotions and sharing them.

Here are several ways you can demonstrate empathy:

By listening with curiosity, speaking with candor, and acting with integrity.

Listening and curiosity allow relationships to thrive. Speaking the truth allows members to be honest with themselves and with you. Acting with integrity keeps relationships on a high standard.

Relationships need curiosity to grow, candor
to deepen, and integrity to endure.

How do your tone of voice and body language affect respect?

Respect can be felt by your tone of voice and body language - how you treat others. Do you listen and ask questions to ensure you understand?

Appreciate those who supported you, forgive those that don't, and help those in need of help.

To empathize with someone means helping them elaborate their feelings.

After a member expresses themselves, see if you can help them elaborate a bit about what they're feeling and why. For example, you might ask, "I imagine you're feeling pretty hurt?" This shows that their feelings matter, and you're trying to understand.

By asking them to elaborate on their feelings.

This allows them to process what they're feeling. Most people just want someone to listen to them.

By not offering advice unless it's asked for.

Skip the unsolicited advice. Many times, when people tell you about a problem, they just want to be heard. Before saying, "just ignore them," be a good listener first. Listen more closely to what they're saying. They need to process their emotions. If you want to help, listen to the whole story and validate their feelings along the way.

Empathy isn't a skill you're born with, but it can be learned to help you in your relationships.

17
BY DEMONSTRATING INTERDEPENDENCE

"The key to growth is the introduction of higher dimensions of consciousness into our awareness."
- Lao Tzu

For some of us, the concept of self-reliance and interdependence are confusing. Self-reliance, to some people, means doing everything yourself and never asking for help. And often, your pride keeps you from asking for help, like when you've been laid off and are looking for work.

Interdependence means doing all you can do and asking for help on what you cannot do, what you cannot do well, or what you don't have time to do because of other priorities.

Self-reliance is a dependence on your capabilities, judgment (Appendix A), or resources. Interdependence is mutual dependence.

What are the four most important human dependencies?

- **Dependence:** From your birth, you were dependent (YOU) on others for your existence.

- **Independence:** Somewhere in your teens, you thought and acted like you were independent (I) - until you learned the truth.

- **Co-Dependence:** Then, some of us become co-dependent, which means we put aside our well-being to maintain a relationship with another. An example is when your spouse is addicted to drugs, and you passively accommodate his addiction to maintain the relationship.

- **Interdependence:** Sometime later in life, you finally realize you can't do it all and transition to interdependence (WE).

Interdependence is the most mature form of dependency.

When you become interdependent, you're well on your way to becoming a *Fully Functioning Adult*. It's the highest form of maturity.

Interdependence means "mutual or concurrent dependence" where all members of a group need each other. It's used to indicate that no one is truly self-sufficient. Interdependence is the mutual reliance between two or more members or groups.

In relationships, interdependence is the degree to which members are mutually dependent on others.

Interdependence in effective teams is where members understand that both personal and team goals are best accomplished with mutual support.

Time isn't wasted over turf problems or attempts for personal gain at the expense of others. The healthiest and most productive way you can interact with others is by being truly interdependent.

18
BY DEMONSTRATING RESILIENCE

"You just can't beat the person who never gives up."
- Babe Ruth

What's resilience, and why is it important? In this assessment, you'll assess the *resiliency* of your career.

Career Resiliency is your ability to bounce back from setbacks, problems, and job loss.

The only way to assess your career and how much risk you're taking is to measure your career resiliency by completing this assessment.

Career Resiliency Assessment

Instructions: Select a number (1 - 4), using the legend below, that most closely represents your agreement or disagreement with each statement below. Place your number to the right of each question. When finished, add your total score.

Legend:
1 = Strongly Disagree; 2 = Disagree; 3 = Agree; 4 = Strongly Agree

My resume communicates my future potential/value (____)

I have written both short and long-range career goals (____)

I can describe my skills and strengths with success stories (____)

I have a coach who can assist me through a career transition (____)

I have good negotiating skills and know what I'm worth (____)

I can answer liability questions (no experience, no degree) (____)

I have a marketing plan developed for my career advancement (____)

I have good relationships outside my unit with suppliers (____)

I believe in my company's leadership, ethics, and integrity (____)

I believe in my company's products and services (____)

My skills have changed to keep pace with my profession (____)

I'm the best in my company at what I do (____)

I have experience in a foreign country (includes Mexico) (____)

I recommend cost-saving and income-producing measures (____)

I maintain relationships with recruiters in my profession (____)

I seek out training that enhances my knowledge and skills (____)

My pay and benefits are above average for my profession (____)

I'm challenged at work for my knowledge, skills, and abilities (____)

I use a computer daily to produce letters, spreadsheets (____)

I am happy with my career and expect to be promoted soon (____)

I am active in association or society representing my profession (____)

I've completed education: AD=1, BD=2, Master=3, PhD=4 (____)

I read one book a month about my chosen profession/function (____)

I have six months in salary saved for career interruptions (____)

I'm a good communicator, both verbally and in writing (____)

I'm constantly seeking ways to develop myself professionally (____)

I have good interpersonal skills, and I'm a good listener (____)

I'm well respected by my peers, subordinates, and superiors (____)

I seek out new technology that makes my unit more productive (____)

I speak a second language (other than English) (____)

List your total score: ____

By being more resilient, you can shorten your recovery time from a job loss, thereby reducing your cost of lost income, enhancing your peace of mind, and reducing your stress level. Of course, you have no control over your company, your boss, the economy, or the marketplace. But you can control the 30 most important areas of your career resiliency.

Career Resiliency gives you greater income-producing potential and a greater competitive edge.

You'll notice that all these statements are within your direct control; therefore, you can change them anytime you choose. If you're not earning the kind of income you deserve, you'll want to spend some quality time working with these 30 resiliency questions.

Score 60 or less: **Ops!** Your career needs professional help quickly. Find a Career Coach you can trust. Ask friends for suggestions or see your local *Yellow Pages* under Career Development, Job Placement, or Employment for available resources. Focus on the 30-resiliency questions with a score of 2 or less. Create a goal to increase your score for each question. Change the way you think, speak, and act about your career. It will make a major difference.

Score 61 – 90: **Not Bad!** To better prepare for an unscheduled career transition, review each resiliency statement and select those with a score of 2 or less. Then, immediately develop a *Plan of Action* (Appendix E) to focus on improving one score at a time until it becomes at least a 3 (Agree). How do you do that? First, you must be willing to change your thoughts and words and commit to taking some bold new actions (deeds). Then, create a plan and take massive action to improve your career resiliency.

Score: 91 – 120: **Good Job!** Begin a program of self-development to strengthen areas with the lowest scores. Since no one is perfect, focus on any score below 3. Get each score to at least a 3 (Agree). Create a goal to increase your score for each question. If not, you'll have a weakness in your career resiliency that could hurt your income-producing potential, causing difficulty and stress.

Effective people take this assessment annually and change what needs to be changed.

This page is intentionally left blank.

19
BY DEMONSTRATING SENSITIVITY

"I'm not concerned with your liking or disliking me...
All I ask is that you respect me as a human being."
- Jackie Robinson

Sensitivity involves learning how to be respectful and consider the perspectives of others.

Sensitivity in the workplace is about ensuring everyone is treated with respect and kindness, regardless of who they are.

By receiving Sensitivity Training Annually

Sensitivity training is about:

- Respecting each member as an equal and as a human being.

- Involves identifying what's likely to be offensive and developing the ability to sincerely apologize when feelings are hurt (including race, culture, gender, sensitivity, and tolerance.

- Teaches:
  - ✓ Diverse group characteristics and definitions, such as cultural, disability, gender, age, and sexual orientation.
  - ✓ How to identify their individual conflict resolution style, and how their style might differ from others.
  - ✓ How to engage in perspective-taking, so it's easier to appreciate another's point of view and come to a mutual understanding.
  - ✓ Sexual Harassment Prevention and EEOC Courses.
  - ✓ American Disabilities Act (ADA), Multiculturalism, and Conflict Resolution.
  - ✓ Bullying in the Workplace and *Keeping the Peace* (Chapter 10).
  - ✓ Sexual Orientation and Gender Identity in the Workplace.

Federal laws prohibit discrimination and harassment in the workplace based on age, sex, race, religion, national origin, disability, pregnancy, and genetic information. Some state and local laws protect even more.

For me, any form of discrimination, resulting in meanness, unfairness, or abusive behavior is hateful, despicable, and unacceptable for any reason.

Training members on how to prevent workplace discrimination and harassment is nothing less than essential to long-term success. Not only can workplace discrimination and harassment affect productivity, but they can also divert resources from the organization's real focus (a distraction). In addition, unacceptable behavior can also become a liability to your company because of discrimination or harassment lawsuits.

By Apologizing with Remorse

Why is it so hard to say you're sorry or admit a mistake? The answer is simple; you're letting your fear and pride get in your way of doing the right thing.

When you hurt someone's feelings or your behavior was unacceptable, have the moral courage to apologize, say you're sorry, what you're sorry for, offer no excuse, and don't do it again.

Why no excuses? Making excuses diminishes your sincerity and makes you sound like you're trying to hide behind your excuse. You're human, and humans make mistakes. Express your sincere remorse, not guilt. Guilt is acknowledging your unacceptable behavior, while remorse is regretting your actions and taking steps to undo the damage. When your finish, look down, say nothing, and wait for a response. The other person doesn't have to forgive you, but you need to forgive yourself and move forward.

Guilt leads to destructive tendencies, while remorse leads to constructive actions. To be remorseful, you must accept the guilt first.

When you make a mistake, have the moral courage to admit it, fix it, and learn from it.

20
BY DEMONSTRATING
HUMILITY

"Talent is God-given. Be humble. Fame is man-given.
Be grateful. Conceit is self-given. Be careful."
- John Wooden

What is humility, its definition, importance, how is it acquired, and where does it come from?

Humility is a deep awareness of unworthiness, not worthlessness.

In my life, humility has always been the character trait I admire most and have the least. I always thought that humility and kindness were synonymous with weakness. It wasn't until much later in life that I realized my error.

You can be kind and humble and still be tough.

Effective people understand and practice the *Power of Humility*. In a religious context, humility can mean recognizing God, accepting one's defects, and submitting to divine grace as a member. Humility is a virtue in many religious and philosophical traditions, often in contrast to narcissism, hubris, and other forms of pride.

In a non-religious context, humility is the self-restraint from excessive vanity and can possess moral and ethical dimensions.

The opposite of humility is bad pride,
the Sin of the Self-Righteous.

Those who are humble respect their limits, admit their mistakes, practice more forgiveness, understand and feel compassion, are less judgmental, cease being self-righteous, live their lives in the present, forget about re-living the past, trust more, let go more easily, are more patient, and are more human. The key to becoming more effective is to treat others with respect and kindness, which requires humility.

Humility includes self-understanding and awareness, openness, perspective-taking. It helps you better understand the human condition of those around you. No one is born with humility. It's something we develop as a result of our actions and intentions. Humility is a character trait you earn by treating others with respect and kindness.

> *If you are humble, nothing will touch you, neither praise*
> *nor disgrace, because you know what you are."*
> *- Mother Teresa*

Humility is the most important trait because it enables patience, forgiveness, and compassion.

Here are the most important things you can do to practice humility:

By being grateful.

Rejoice in your existence, count your blessings, be grateful for the gift of life, and be grateful for winning the Lottery-being born in America rather than Somalia.

By admitting you don't know everything.

Humbleness helps you better understand the human condition of those around you. Just because you think you're right doesn't make you superior. Humble yourself by asking better questions and admitting that you don't know everything. Understanding, like knowledge, is relative; just when you think you know it all - it changes.

Effective people take the blame for the failure and give away the credit for success.

By not trying to prove you're right all the time.

Which is more important, being right or your relationship with others? Just because you think you're right doesn't make you superior. Sometimes you're so blinded by your pride that you completely forget about the damage you're doing to your relationships by trying to prove you're right. It takes humility to admit that others are better than you.

If you don't humble yourself, someone will do it for you.

By learning how to agree-to-disagree.

This is all about situational awareness, your sensitivity to nurturing good relations – regardless of who's right or wrong. Instead of trying to win every argument, you could say, *"I respectfully disagree, but please help me understand why you feel the way you do?"* Then, listen intently because you might just learn something.

Now share why you feel the way you do and look for common ground to move forward. If things get heated, take a break, and come back later.

By getting lost in the service of others (Chapter 37).

By accepting your weaknesses.

Everyone has weaknesses. For those of you who think you have no weaknesses, that thought by itself becomes your weakness because it leads to pride and arrogance. Your weaknesses help you stay humble.

By counting your blessings.

We are all blessed beyond measure. If you were born and live in America, you've won the lottery! Of all the billions of people on the earth, how did you get so lucky? The right intent must accompany your actions. When you are truly grateful, you will receive the gift of humility, which will bless your life.

By being teachable.

Without humility, you're unteachable because you're unwilling to learn. Your Pride and Fear are preventing you from learning. Accept feedback from others. Learn from criticism and the opinions of others. You get to choose what to do with it. But seek it and use it to become more effective.

By demonstrating inclusiveness.

Inclusiveness is your ability to let people in and make them feel welcome. Diversity and inclusion are critical elements of every recruitment and retention program. Diversity in the workplace means that a company employs a diverse team of people that reflect the society in which it exists. Inclusion exists when all members are treated fairly and respectfully, have equal access to opportunities and resources, and can contribute fully to the company's success.

By getting your fear and pride out of your way.

Accept and allow others' strengths to work for the good of the team without interference. Let members do their jobs. It's not about you-it's about them. Your micro-managing will destroy the team's morale and your credibility. It takes humility to admit that your way isn't always the best.

By being patient.

Developing sincere humility is a process, not something created overnight. Through diligence and faith, it can be done, and it's worth it! Without humility, you'll never have self-awareness, perspective, openness to feedback and ideas, and an appreciation of others. Without humility, you'll never be effective, period!

By being vulnerable.

A big part of building lasting relationships is the willingness to be vulnerable and authentic. Typically, this means being open to new ideas, stepping outside of comfort zones (Chapter 13), and being transparent about your mistakes and shortcomings.

> *"Vulnerability sounds like truth and feels like courage. Truth and courage aren't always comfortable, but they're never weakness."*
> *- Brené Brown*

When team members are vulnerable to each other, it builds trust. In turn, they're more comfortable and confident about being open with their questions, sharing new ideas, debating and discussing challenges, and expressing differences of opinion. This enables stronger team performance. Be humble enough to suspend your agendas and judgments. You might just learn something. Validate the unique perspectives of others.

Being effective means getting your fear and pride out of your way.

Share your mistakes as teachable moments, engage in dialogue, not debate, and empower others to lead.

By never raising your voice in anger.

Need I say more?

21
BY GIVING AND
RECEIVING FEEDBACK

"Feedback is the Breakfast of Champions"
- Ken Blanchard

Have you ever worked for someone who seldom told you how you were doing? How did that make you feel? If you're looking to improve your performance or the performance of others, feedback helps to make the adjustments and corrections needed.

What's Feedback?

The goal of feedback is to identify the gap between <u>desired</u> and <u>actual</u> performance (for results and behavior) of members, teams, units, and systems) and to close the gap ASAP.

If you don't receive feedback, ask for it;

not only from your boss but from others.

Feedback can occur anytime but normally comes during audits, performance-oriented training, performance appraisals and reviews, shareholders' meetings, marketing research, 360-degree feedback, peak performance coaching, visits and observations, on-site inspections, surveys, meetings, and *After-Action Reviews.*

What's the Feedback Loop for Human Performance?

Here are the most important steps of the *Feedback Loop.*

Step 1: Evidence: The performance must be measured, recorded, and assessed.

Step 2: Relevance: Feedback must be relayed to the member in a context that makes sense.

Step 3: Consequence: Feedback must illuminate a path to improvement.

Step 4: Action: Members must change their <u>actual</u> performance to come closer to the <u>desired</u> performance.

Then, that new performance can be re-measured, and the feedback loop can run once more, every action stimulating new performance that moves the member closer to the underlined desired performance.

How do you give Feedback?

If you fail to provide periodic and specific feedback to your members, your silence will speak louder than words. It's your job to let them know how they're doing.

If your feedback is positive, share it with everyone publicly. If your feedback is negative, do so in private. Take a moment to ensure the member knew the correct standard and didn't have a good reason for doing (or failing to do) what he did.

However, giving someone your opinion doesn't constitute feedback unless they act on your opinion and thus cause you to revise it.

How do you receive Feedback?

When you receive feedback, you get to decide how you'll respond and if you'll use it to become more effective. Unfortunately, feedback is often perceived as a euphemism for criticism. If you "blow it off," you'll never get any better. You don't have to agree. Initially, you won't. However, arguing or being defensive sends the wrong message.

Humble yourself! Remember, no matter how painful, you need the feedback because you'll never become more effective or successful without it. Also, the person giving the feedback might someday be in a position to shape your future.

So, be *self-correcting*! Prove that you're listening and getting better every day (Appendix G).

Effective people thrive on feedback because their goal is to become more effective and successful.

If you fail to give and receive feedback, expect that you'll never be accused of adding value to others or being self-correcting.

22
BY ASSESSING
PERFORMANCE

"Followership, like leadership, is a role and not a destination."
- Michael McKinney

How will your boss assess your performance? Are they getting better or worse? How do you know for sure? Your performance includes your results, behavior, and potential.

Effective people don't just set the bar; they are the bar.

Are they getting better or worse? How do you know for sure?

What's the best way to assess performance?

The best way to assess performance is by using solid, objective measurements. Actual performance measurement is a more effective way to evaluate results because the measurement is relevant to the situation or process.

Some of the best ways to assess performance are by using *Metrics, Objectives and Key Results (OKRs)*, *Key Performance Indicators (KPIs), and Bands of Excellence (BOEs).*

By using Metrics

Metrics are quantifiable and allow you to set the <u>desired</u> result compared to the <u>actual</u> result, but there's a downside.

A metric is something used to measure and track the results of members, teams, or systems to assess its performance.

Here's a good story:

Bob was assigned to improve the number of "problem fixes per day" called into the Helpdesk in his company. He spent a few hours in the Helpdesk Call Center to observe. To his amazement, he found that each Helpdesk Operator was assessed daily using 17 different metrics. One metric was how much "time the operator spent on the phone."

The operators were told to keep each call to less than two minutes, which was counterproductive in solving the caller's problems. After a few hours, Bob determined that working under these conditions (metrics) was not where he wanted to work. His intuition told him that the metrics were too restrictive. He directed that all metrics be stopped except for one; the number of "problems fixed per day."

Result? The number of *"problems fixed per day"* shot up off the charts. Problem solved! So, be careful with all your metrics. Sometimes less is more. Focus on the most important metrics – the ones that make sense.

Here are some typical metrics.

- **Cash Flow:** Cash flow is the money coming in and out of your business on any given day, which is what you use to cover your business expenses, such as payroll, rent, and inventory.

- **Customer: Customer Acquisition Cost (CAC).** Divide your total acquisition costs by the number of new customers over the same time frame you're examining.

- **Employee: Employee Turnover Rate (ETR).** To determine your ETR, take the number of employees who have departed the company and divide it by the average number of employees. If you have a high ETR, spend some time examining your workplace culture, employment packages, and work environment.

By using Objectives and Key Results (OKRs)

Objectives and Key Results (or OKRs) are a framework for defining and tracking objectives and their outcomes.

OKRs are generally attributed to **Andy Grove**, CEO of Intel, who introduced the approach to Intel during his tenure there and documented this in his 1983 book *High Output Management*. OKRs comprise an Objective, a clearly defined goal, and one or more **K**ey **R**esults (specific measures used to track the achievement of that objective).

OKRs:

- May be shared across the company to provide teams with visibility of goals to align and focus effort.

- Are typically set at the company, team, and personal levels, although there is criticism on this causing too much of a waterfall approach, which OKRs try to be the opposite.

- Overlap with other performance management frameworks - complexity sitting somewhere between KPI and the balanced scorecard.

The idea took hold, and OKRs quickly became central to Google's culture as a "management methodology" that helps ensure that the company focuses effort on the same important issues throughout the company."

Since becoming popular at Google, OKR has favored several similar tech start-ups, including LinkedIn, Twitter, and Uber. For more on OKRs, review the book or audiobook, *Measure What Matters* by **John Doerr.**

By using Key Performance Indicators (KPIs)

KPIs provide a company with a focus for strategic and operational improvement and compare achievements to similar companies.

A Key Performance Indicator (KPI) is a performance measure that demonstrates how effectively a company is at achieving its key objectives.

To be effective, a *KPI* must be well-defined and quantifiable, communicated throughout your company, crucial to achieving the goal, and applicable to the business.

Here's the difference between a *Metric* and a *KPI?*

- *KPIs* support business goals and objectives.

- *Metrics* support *KPIs* and focus on the overall tactical business goals and objectives.

Meaningful performance measures start with measurable goals. This means that your goal needs to be clear enough that you can imagine how you'll recognize it when it becomes real. So, you might first want to check if your current goals are measurable. Members won't *buy in* to something they don't understand, weren't involved, and see no relevance. The key to deriving *KPIs* from objectives is to work backward and reverse engineer the *metrics* you want to create. This process is called goal, question, metric. Your objectives are your goals for your business or project.

By using Bands of Excellence (BOEs)

Since *Public-Sector Organizations,* like teachers or government workers, don't focus on profit generation, what matters most to their survival is providing a service that serves the greater good (like schools and government agencies). But how do they do that?

They use a metric called a *Band of Excellence (or BOE)* to measure and assess their level of services. Those who work in the Public-Sector must maintain their *Band of Excellence (BOE)* set by their organization. Think of *BOEs* as the desired Standard of Performance for members, units, and systems.

A Band of Excellence is a set of performance limits ranging from the Minimum (or Standard) performance limit to the Maximum performance limit.

The difference between the minimum and the maximum is called the *Band of Excellence.* If your performance stays within the *Band of Excellence,* you remain employable. Here's a simple example.

The biggest government agency on the planet is the US Department of Defense. In 1992, as a former US Army Officer, here's the BOE used to

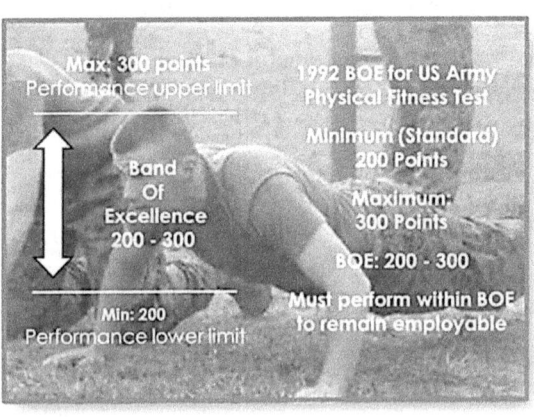

measure physical fitness by taking the Annual Physical Fitness Test.

The BOE Minimum (or Standard) was 200 points overall. The BOE Maximum was 300 points overall. The BOE was 200 - 300 for the test overall to remain promotable. If a Soldier failed to achieve 200 points overall, he was retrained and retested. If he failed a second time, he was considered un-promotable and processed for release from the military.

Have you ever tried to measure how you and your unit were doing? If not, you will. In every viable business, key metrics help determine the answer to one simple question: Are we getting better *Over-Time*?

Over-time means as compared to a

past time (last month or year).

And ask the same question about yourself, *are you getting better over-time?* And your business unit, *is my business unit getting better over-time?* But how can you tell?

Here's a good example:

Think of *KPIs* as your Doctor does when you go for a physical.

- **Step 1:** What gets measured? They measure the most important aspects of optimum health, like weight, height, blood pressure, pulse, temperature, and cholesterol.

- **Step 2:** If this is your first physical, how do your numbers compare to a healthy person your age (what's the norm, standard, or benchmark)? Any corrective action needed?

- **Step 3:** If this isn't your first physical, how do your numbers compare to your last physical? Are you (your physical system) getting better *over-time*? Any corrective action needed?

Use this same process with all your *Key Performance Indicators*. What are the things you can measure that tell you about the health of your unit?

Are you getting better over-time?

If not, why? What can be done (corrective action) to reverse the numbers? What number is acceptable to you? What are your standards? If this number rises above or falls below a certain level, what corrective action must be taken? Trends.

One way to visually track your *KPIs* is to measure and compare your numbers *over-time*, the trend. What does the trend look like? Is it trending in the right direction? By doing so, you'll be able to see if the trend is getting better or worse.

Here's an example of Tracking Trends.

Accounts Receivable, 90-Days Past Due (As of June 21, 20XX)			
This month	Last month	2-Months ago	1-Year Ago
$15,335	$12,457	$10,237	$25,936

Notice that this table is tracking a *Key Performance Indicator* that measures *Accounts Receivable over a 90-day period.* The current status ("This Month") is greater than last month and the month before. In other words, your *90-Day Past Due* numbers are increasing or getting worse.

Tip: Check the usage rate or consumption rate metrics for your unit over-time and see what you learn.

23
BY ASSESSING
RESULTS

"Incremental progress leads to long-lasting results."
- Frank Sonnenberg

How will your boss measure your results? Your performance includes your results, behavior, and potential. Results deal with what the member achieved and include actual job outputs, countable products, measurable outcomes, and accomplishments. They're normally measured objectively (with numbers and metrics), but not always. Member results don't have to be observed, which means that the result could be a mental result, like an answer or a decision. However, the result must be something under the member's control, regardless of whether the result is mental or physical.

Self-Test
Do your Results Support your Boss?

Effective people have a strong sense of duty, do the right thing at the right time, and don't need prodding or reminding.

Here are the most common expectations of your results.

1. Are you *accountable* for your results and the consequences?

2. Do you help your boss achieve his goals, no matter what?

3. Do you consistently produce excellent results?

4. Do you always do your best work?

5. Do you know all that's expected of you?

6. Do you consistently get things done the right way the first time?

7. Can you be counted on to get things done without direct supervision?

8. Do you proactively anticipate problems?

9. Are you self-correcting?

10. Do you catch errors and mistakes before your boss?

11. Do you recommend solutions to your boss?

12. Do you continuously seek ways to improve what you do?

13. Are you improving your skills through training?

14. Do you ensure your boss is the first to hear any bad news?

15. If you don't know, do you ask?

16. If you're supposed to know something but don't, do you find out and follow-through ASAP?

17. Do you contribute to your boss's meetings, activities, and events?

18. Do you cease discussion when your boss makes the final decision?

19. Do you support your boss's decisions, as your decision, especially if you disagree?

20. Do you ensure your focus and priorities reinforce your boss's?

21. Do you know your boss's intent, responsibilities, expectations, projects, goals, and standards?

22. Do you know your boss's values, priorities, and idiosyncrasies?

23. Do you have access to information sharing and processing?

24. Do you have permission to voice your honest opinion, behind closed doors, without fear of negative consequences?

25. Do you avoid last-minute surprises for your boss?

26. Do you keep the boss informed?

27. Do you anticipate and accommodate change?

28. Do you follow up and follow-through?

29. Do you know what matters most to your boss?

30. Do you ask for feedback from your boss and team members?

31. Do you manage your workload and professional development?

32. Do you manage your time, changes, and challenges well?

If you answered NO to five or more of these questions, you need to reassess your results and change what needs to be changed. Effective people take this assessment annually to demonstrate that they're *self-correcting* (Appendix G).

24
BY ASSESSING
BEHAVIOR

"If a man aspires to the highest place, it is no
dishonor to him to halt at the second."
- Cicero

How will your boss assess your behavior? Your behavior includes your competencies, skills, attitude, expertise, and proficiencies, the adherence to organizational values, customer feedback, supplier feedback, and the personal style, manner, and approach used. Behavior is normally assessed subjectively (someone's opinion), but not always.

You're expected to perform your job in a way that reflects positively on the organization's standards and expectations. Your behavior is the sum of everything you say and do, as well as everything you fail to say and do.

Self-Test
Does your Behavior Support your Boss?

Effective people have a strong sense of duty, do the right thing at the right time, and don't need prodding or reminding.

Here are the most common expectations of your behavior.

1. Do you treat everyone with respect and kindness?

2. Are you *accountable* for your behavior and the consequences?

3. Do you add value to all those who help you achieve your results?

4. Do you play by the rules unless you have a good reason for not doing so?

5. Do you demonstrate a positive attitude?

6. Do you avoid gossiping and speaking badly of others unless in your boss's office, privately?

7. Are you a team player?

8. Do you fully cooperate, coordinate, and collaborate?

9. Do you stay home and call your boss if you have common signs of being sick?

10. Do you know your boss's expectations of tradition and culture?

11. Do you deal honestly with others - revealing problems and telling the whole story?

12. Do you avoid wasting your boss's time?

13. Do you maintain the standards for behavior?

14. Do you give feedback to your boss?

15. Do you refrain from making excuses? (Appendix G)

16. Do you refrain from complaining and blaming others?

17. Does your behavior reflect positively on your company?

18. Do you demonstrate *accountability* (Appendix G)?

19. Do you communicate well with customers and team members?

20. Do you adhere to all restrictions, policies, and procedures?

21. Does your behavior contribute to the stability, harmony, integrity, or cohesiveness of your team?

If you answered NO to three or more of these questions, you need to reassess your behavior and change what needs to be changed. Effective people take this assessment annually to demonstrate that they're *self-correcting* (Appendix G).

25
BY CONDUCTING A
PERFORMANCE REVIEW

"What we can control is our performance and our execution,
and that's what we're going to focus on."
- Bill Belichick

Performance reviews are a form of feedback, but they're normally given once a year in writing. If you wait a year to provide feedback to your team members, you have done them a grave disservice.

They all need to know how they're doing at least quarterly.

One of the most important things you can do is coach your team members to either reinforce their actions and results or redirect their actions.

Here's an example of what you might do.

Member's Self-Assessment

Performance coaching should start by asking for a self-assessment like:

"John, tell me how you think your unit has been performing."

"Is there any room for improvement?"

"How do you measure their progress, their
results vs. the desired outcome?"

"How about a self-assessment; how do you think you're doing?"

"Any room for self-improvement?"

Note: Some *organizations even formalize the process by asking members to fill out a written self-assessment before the session.

*To learn more about ***Organizing***, available at **Amazon.com,** see page 5.

Boss's Assessment

Phase 1: Present the Positives.

Listen carefully, take notes, and ask thoughtful questions. When you begin your assessment, start by saying,

"Do you know what I really like about you? You're... "

Present all the positives.

Phase 2: Discuss a few things you'd like them to work on.

When ready to provide any constructive feedback, start by saying,

"There're a few small things I'd like you to work on. ......"

This way, you reinforce the positive and assign a few small things to work on in the future.

Phase 3: Goal Setting.

*"Let's set some stretch goals for you to meet
for our next meeting. What's fair?"*

Now, negotiate his goals; not too easy, but not too hard. You are building him up for success, not failure (Appendix C). Feedback is critical to everyone's development. It helps close the gap between actual and desired performance. Without it, your members are operating in the dark.

Phase 4: Personal Growth.

How's your personal growth plan for your career coming?

Since achieving your true potential isn't by accident, what intentional actions are you taking to improve your career?

Document the response for the next review. Provide support as needed.

26
BY COACHING FOR
PEAK PERFORMANCE

"Failure is good. It's fertilizer. Everything I've learned
about coaching, I've learned from making mistakes."
- Rick Pitino

Effective people know that coaching is a results-oriented, quality-focused process and a *cutting-edge* system to improve personal and team effectiveness. A Coach is a facilitator, guide, and strategic resource who demonstrates perceptiveness, integrity, and truth-telling in supporting the member's progress towards his self-determined objectives.

Ask more, Tell less!

The coach facilitates the member's growth through a series of *Socratic* questioning (deductive) and doesn't profess to have all the answers. However, mutual accountability and trust and the depth of the coach's experience give the process its power and effectiveness.

Here are the three most important features that make coaching work.

Synergy: Here, the member and the Coach become a team by focusing on the member's goals and needs and accomplishing more than the member would alone.

Structure: With a Coach, a member takes more actions, thinks bigger, and gets the job done due to the accountability the Coach encourages

Expertise: The Coach has some knowledge or experiences the member needs.

What's the Coach's Job?

Help the member establish written goals.

Turn breakdowns into breakthroughs.

Encourage accountability.

Teach or mentor.

Help the member make a quantum leap.

What's the Team Member's Job?

Tell the truth.

Be prepared.

Stay in action.

Be on time for conversations.

Be accountable.

Coaching is a system centered on listening, asking, leading, and honoring. Coaching is not telling or supervising. It's different. Coaching doesn't encourage co-dependency, lack of accountability, or making excuses. It encourages just the opposite.

What Tools does a Coach use?

Listening: So, the member feels heard and supported.

Asking questions: So, the member uncovers his answers.

Requesting actions: So, the member stays on-track.

Intuiting: So, the truth is revealed.

What Format does a Coach use?

Member and coach agree upon an exciting goal.

Member visits coach to check progress.

Conversations are limited to no more than one hour

Both have an agenda for each conversation.

Member tracks results for reporting to the Coach.

What does the Coach ask during each session?

What was your intended goal?

How far along should you be by today?

Where are you?

What were your obstacles?

What were your accomplishments?

What's your plan going forward?

What're you keeping a secret and not telling me?

What Techniques does a Coach use?

Coaching is a wonderful skill. The coaching skill we're referring to is asking better questions to have the member come to his own conclusions and solutions. The easiest way to explain coaching techniques is to use the example of **Dr. Phil McGraw**. He uses reality therapy along with the *Insanity Test, the Truth Test, and the Take-away.*

The Insanity Test:

Have you ever been guilty of insane behavior? We all have on many occasions.

Insane behavior is doing the same thing over and over again while expecting a different result.

The Truth Test:

The *Truth Test* is when *Dr. Phil* asks his clients,

"How's that workin out for ya?"

If what you've been doing isn't producing the results you're seeking, then why are you still doing the same old thing? Why not try something new?

"What do you need to do?"

These questions help the member come to his conclusions. This process is desirable because the member is the one who must execute the solution. If he came up with the solution on his own, he'd be much more likely to take ownership of the solution.

This is coaching at its best, asking better questions and letting the other person decide what needs to be done. If they have no clue what to do, offer suggestions, but let them decide what needs to be done.

Then, get them to commit to a *Plan of Action* over a specified period and reassess their results. Then, adjust from there.

When you tell someone what to do, that's consulting or advising, but certainly not coaching.

The Take-Away:

This is a powerful technique and uses the withdrawal of something, which taps into their innate *fear of loss* and sounds something like this:

> *"This is probably not right for you."*

> *"You probably wouldn't qualify."*

> *"The timing for you to do this is probably not the best right now."*

> *"I don't think this is going to work for you."*

It normally generates a response like, "What do you mean? What's wrong with me? Why wouldn't I qualify?"

Now, you've got their interest because no one wants to lose anything – even if they don't have it yet. Now they want it more. Make sense?

In this case, the Coach could withdraw his coaching.

27

BY USING
AFFIRMATIONS & VISUALIZATION

*"We must concentrate not merely on the negative expulsion
of war but the positive affirmation of peace."*
- Martin Luther King, Jr.

Affirmations are intended to help you unleash the personal power you
never thought you had.

**An affirmation is a short and uplifting
statement that is declared by you to be true.**

For example, when your conscious mind vividly imagines that you are a
great public speaker, your unconscious mind must now produce evidence
to support this new thought through a combination of visualization and
positive affirmations.

To truly see, you must first sincerely believe it exists.

The unconscious mind now thinks that you're a great public speaker.

So, how does this manifest? First, through new behavior, like new thoughts
and ideas, questions, energy, and motivation, you'll:

- Find yourself associating with others who are good speakers.

- Want to read books, listen to audio, and watch videos about
  speaking.

- Attend seminars and workshops on how to sharpen your skills at
  publicly speaking.

This *self-fulfilling prophecy,* combined with education, training, and
practice, will lower your anxiety level. And through all this, you'll find
that the best public speakers still get nervous and anxious just before they
begin every speaking engagement-just like you. What's the difference?

Their feelings are processed differently. How do you know what to focus
on? What's important? Since you're bombarded by billions of bits of data
every day, your mind makes decisions for you.

A small portion of your brain, located at the base of the brain stem about the size and shape of a quarter of an apple, called the *Reticular Activating System* (or RAS), decides what you focus on. And who programs your *Reticular Activating System*?

Actually, you do!

Opportunities in life are neutral and don't become more accessible because you think you deserve it, or you've paid your dues.

Concentrate on what you really want. By doing so, you reprogram your subconscious mind. You actively program your RAS (sometimes by default) every day without even knowing it.

Remember the last time you bought a new car? Then, just after you drove it off the lot, you started to notice how many other people were driving a vehicle just like yours. What caused that? You programmed your RAS to notice. Before that time, there were just as many vehicles as yours out on the highway, but you just weren't programmed to notice.

What's the implication here? The principal implication is that opportunities have always been around you in the past, but either you never recognized them as an opportunity (your RAS wasn't programmed), or you recognized the opportunity but didn't feel qualified (Pride) or worthy to receive it (Fear).

Ever wonder why some people achieve greatness in their life, and you're still waiting? Those who've achieved greatness did so because they could create a clear and positive view of how they wanted their life to turn out.

Your vision of your life can be achieved if you know what you want, really believe you can get there, and never give up. One way to achieve this is by creating and using your personal affirmation.

Here's an example of a *Personal Affirmation* for someone whose most important goal is to get a college education.

"I've decided to improve my life regardless of my circumstances.

Goal Example: *I enjoy the confidence I feel from earning my Bachelor's Degree in Engineering from ABC University because I know it will help me achieve my true potential.*

I accept full responsibility for my success, and I'll make no excuses. I know that good things are supposed to happen to me. I welcome the opportunity to learn new things and become a better person. I will work hard to achieve an 'A' in all my classes.

My pursuit of excellence inspires me to study, research, and master the material my instructors present. Every subject is important to me, no matter how difficult. I will complete all assigned work daily before taking time for recreation. I take my studies seriously!

It's possible for me to live my dreams and to help others to do the same. No matter how bad it gets, I know that I'll make it because I've got the right stuff. I'm hungry for a better life. I believe that it's far better to be prepared and have no opportunity than to have an opportunity and be unprepared. I'll always be prepared because I want success more than anyone.

To this end, I'll endure all things and refuse to give up or to give in until I win. Failure isn't an option for me. I know that I can do all things through God, who strengthens me.

This is one example of a personal affirmation for someone whose goal is to get a college education. After you've written your affirmation, using your words, read your affirmation aloud at least three times daily - when you awake, during lunch, and just before you go to bed.

Do this for thirty days, and those around you will notice that you have a new attitude. This new attitude will be the foundation to propel you forward and to take the actions necessary to get you where you want to be.

The Power of Visualization

"I believe that visualization is one of the most powerful means of achieving personal goals."
- Harvey Mackay.

Visualization is a powerful tool that begins with a picture or sketch of something tangible you're trying to achieve.

Visualization taps into your unconscious mind due to the power of expectations because you get what you expect from life.

Visualization is powerful because it helps program your subconscious mind.

This picture is an example of visualization for a young woman whose goal is to get a college education.

By constantly seeing this picture, your unconscious mind suggests to your conscious mind new and innovative ways to help manifest that which you're seeking. Post your picture on your mirror, in your car, on your desk, and anywhere else so you will see it several times every day. Better yet, put your face into the picture!

Visualization creates a clearer picture of where you're going, enhancing the belief in your ability to get there, creating motivation and excitement in reaching your objective and a greater sense of purpose and focus.

The greatest obstacles to *affirmations* and *visualization* are self-doubt, uncertainty, pride, fear, and miscommunications. What picture could represent your goal? What does your visualization look like?

28
BY COMMITTING
TO PURPOSE

*"Concerning all acts of initiative and creation, there is
one elementary truth – that the moment one definitely
commits oneself, then Providence moves, too."*
- Goethe

A commitment is a duty, obligation, or responsibility, a promise or agreement to do something in the future, being bound emotionally or intellectually to a course of action or another person. It affects your effectiveness by how your treat your team members and how they work together.

People who've *committed to purpose* do their best and get things done the right way the first time. They don't complain or gossip, ask for feedback from others and take personal responsibility and accountability (Appendix G) for their actions and the consequences (Appendix F).

Committing to purpose means mentally accepting
your situation and making the best of it.

Your purpose comes from letting go of your need to question, complain, or argue and to move toward total cooperation. You're *all in,* and there is no turning back because you've *burned-all-your-bridges.*

An excellent example is **Mother Teresa,** who never complained about having to work in the slums of Calcutta. Instead, she accepted her situation and did her best to ease the pain and suffering - one soul at a time. She was in an impossible situation that she knew she couldn't change.

If you want committed team members,

give them meaningful assignments, encouragement,

support, and recognition.

Commitment requires action. You can say you're committed, but the proof is in what you've done.

How do you know if you're committed to purpose?

The next time you enjoy Ham and Eggs for breakfast, stop to remember that the Chicken was involved, but the Pig was committed!

You know you've *committed to purpose* when you let go of all the negatives (Fear and Pride) that have been holding you back, completely accept who you are and what you're doing, disengage from your struggles, no longer question or complain, forget about yourself, and resolve to fully cooperate without hesitation.

When this happens, you've arrived; you've *committed to purpose*.

I'm a living witness to the power of committing to purpose in my life. It's the most effective way I know of to achieve your goals.

29
BY BUILDING
EFFECTIVE TEAMS

"A team is a small number of people with complementary skills who are committed to a common purpose, set of performance goals, and approach for which they hold themselves mutually accountable."
- The Leadership Edge

Do you know how to build effective teams to consistently produce excellent results?

Team Building is a process of clarifying goals, building ownership across the team, and identifying obstacles and risks, and eliminating or mitigating them.

Effective people know that effective teams are the building blocks of greatness. The purpose of assembling a team is to accomplish bigger goals than any members could achieve working alone. Create a conversation between your team and your #1 customer to gain commitment, clarity, and alignment.

What are the most important things teams need to be effective?

- Strong leadership and common goals.
- Rules of the game (things they must do and must not do).
- A *Plan Of Action* (POA) and support for risk-taking.
- 100% involvement and inclusion (access to information).
- Empowerment to overcome obstacles and distractions.
- To be held accountable for their results (Appendix D).

What questions should every member be able to answer?

- What's the team's purpose?
- Why's this purpose important, and whom do they serve?
- What're the key things they deliver?
- What happens if they can't deliver these things?
- What does a "Win" look like for the team?

The purpose of a team is to perform, get results and achieve victory in the workplace; to win! Effective people gather groups of members and mold them into proactive and productive teams.

Effective teams are the building blocks of greatness.

What are the most important behaviors of effective teams?

- **Commitment:** Only those committed to excellence are hired. New members are selected by the team based on their hard and soft skills. Everyone works together, like in a Fire House.
- **Communications:** Members practice open and honest communications and understand each other's points of view.
- **Contributions:** They contribute to the team's success by applying their unique talents, knowledge, and creativity.
- **Cooperation:** Each member recognizes that conflict is a normal part of doing business. They view these situations as an opportunity for new ideas and creativity. They work to resolve conflict quickly and constructively.
- **Development:** They're encouraged to continually learn new skills and apply what they've learned on the job. They believe they have the support of the team.
- **Decision-making:** All participate in decisions affecting the team. But they understand the boss makes the final decision. Positive win/win, collaborative results are the goal always. Once the decision is made, they set aside their personal opinions and get to work executing the decision (Appendix B).
- **Interdependence:** Members recognize their interdependence and understand that personal and team goals are best accomplished with mutual support. Time isn't wasted over turf issues or attempts for personal gain at the expense of others.
- **Ownership:** They all feel a sense of ownership because they're committed to values-based common goals, which they create.
- **Structure:** Members work in a structured environment. They know what boundaries exist and who has final authority. The boss sets agreed-upon high standards of performance and is respected via active, willing participation.
- **Trust:** All members work in a climate of trust and are encouraged to openly express ideas, opinions, disagreements, and feelings. Questions are welcomed.

30
BY CONDUCTING
TEAM BUILDING SESSIONS

"Team stands for Together Everyone Achieves More."
– Unknown

Effective bosses know that when starting a new position, it's always a good idea, within the first 30 days, to meet with all Direct Reports to build relationships, solidify team cohesion, and develop a game plan going forward. One way to achieve this is to conduct a *Team Building Session* to establish a baseline.

A Team Building Session is a meeting of all Direct Reports, and their Direct Reports, to synchronizing them in time and space and enhance team cohesion.

This includes goals, vision, mission, priorities, expectations, and *Unresolved Issues* (Appendix E). *Unresolved Issues* will be captured and consolidated into a *Plan of Action* (Appendix E).

Each issue will be assigned a *Champion* to own the issue and report the progress to you monthly until resolved.

It's best to arrange an off-site location (like a hotel, lodge, or resort) over a Friday and Saturday or an entire weekend. This gets team members on an even playing field away from all the pressures of the day.

This is a mandatory event with no exceptions. Invite all team members and their team members from both *Line and Staff* units. You'll also need easels, large sheets of butcher paper, masking tape, and markers to record comments during the session.

These sessions are normally planned and conducted by the number two person who acts as the facilitator.

Here are the most important things you'll need:

- **Self-Introduction Forms:** This form is provided to each attendee, asking them to fill it out in advance and read it as a self-introduction at the beginning of the session.

- **Areas of Concern Survey:** This questionnaire contains a list of questions anonymously completed by each attendee and given to the facilitator two days before the session. All answers are anonymous and are consolidated and presented to the group for discussion.

- **New Boss Presentation:** As a minimum, this is the boss's opportunity to tell team members what's important, what they can expect, what you expect from them, how you feel about exercising initiative, your core values, your vision, your experience, and how you feel about them and their families.

- **Philosophy of Serving:** This is also your opportunity, as the new boss, to inspire and motivate your team right from the start (Chapter 39). You only get one chance to make a good first impression. Make it count!

- **Give them something meaningful:** Give all attendees something that means a great deal to you, like a poem, book, or movie.

What does a 2-day program look like?

Here's an example of a 2-day program for a Team Building Session:

Day 1:	**Day 2:**
Introduction: Facilitator	*Breakfast:*
Self-introductions: 3-5 minutes each	Break-out sessions to *Brainstorm* options to deal with concerns and *Unresolved Issues*: Facilitator
Lunch:	
Review Areas of Concern: Facilitator	*Lunch:*
Identify *Unresolved Issues*: Facilitator	Groups present recommendations: Group leaders
	Concluding Remarks: New boss
Dinner/Social:	

Note: In the end, assign each concern or *Unresolved Issue* to a team member to create a *Plan of Action* (Appendix E).

What does a Self-Introduction Form look like?

Instructions: Complete this form and bring it with you to the *Team Building Session.*

- I am (name), and I'm the (title). I've held this position since____.

- My background and experience are ____.

- The one thing I like best about my job is____.

- The one thing I like least is____.

- I consider my leadership style to be____.

- During my non-work time, I like to ____.

- The one thing my unit does best is____.

- The one thing my unit needs to work on is _____.

- The top three priorities for my unit are ____.

- My single greatest concern is _____.

- I consider my strengths to be _____.

- My weaknesses are ____.

- My goal in this position is ____.

What does an Area of Concern Survey look like?

<u>Instructions:</u> Complete this form and return it to _____, no later than two days before the *Team Building Session.* Your answers will be kept confidential, consolidated, and presented for discussion during the session. The term Organization is the unit the new boss is leading.

Here are the most important questions to answer:

- What does this Organization do best?

- What does this Organization do worst?

- What programs, policies, products, or services should be started, stopped, or changed, and why?

- What trends or changes have you seen as important to sustain the Organization for the next 5-10 years?

- What should the Organization's top three priorities be?

- How would you describe what this Organization does in one sentence?

- How would you describe this Organization's #1 customer?

- What other customers could use this Organization's products or services?

- If you were the boss of this Organization, what would you do to improve profitability?

- What are this Organization's top three problems or threats?

- The most important thing that's not working is ____.

- What are this Organization's top three strengths and opportunities?

- What do you want to know about your new boss?

- Any other comments or suggestions?

<u>Note:</u> It's also a good idea to conduct this activity once a year, or when changes occur, to keep everyone synchronized. You can also invite spouses and schedule tours and shopping for them.

What one thing could you give them that has meaning in your life?

Winners and Losers

A winner says: Let's find out.
A loser says: Nobody knows.
When a winner makes a mistake, he says: I was wrong.
When a loser makes a mistake, he says: It wasn't my fault.
A winner goes through a problem and deals with it.
A loser goes around a problem, and never gets past it.
A winner makes commitments. *A loser makes promises.*
A winner says: I am good, but not as good as I ought to be.
A loser says: I am not as bad as a lot of other people.
A winner tries to learn from those who are superior to him.
A loser tries to tear down those who are superior to him.
A winner says: There ought to be a better way to do it.
A loser says: That's the way it has always been done.
A winner says: I will find the right people who can help me.
A loser says: I will do it myself.
A winner looks for an answer in every problem.
A loser looks for a problem in every answer.
A winner says: I will do it now!
A loser says: I will do it later.
A winner says: I will quit trying and simply do.
A loser says: I will keep trying.
A winner says: I will create my own good luck.
A loser says: I might get lucky.
A winner makes things happen.
A loser lets things happen.
-Hannah du Plessis

Are you a Winner or a Loser? Then, act like it!

This page is intentionally left blank.

31
BY BUILDING
TRUST

"Better to trust the man who is frequently in error
than the one who is never in doubt."
- Eric Sevareid

Trust is the glue that holds everything together for any company. Trust is important in business because it forms the basis of all relationships and interactions.

Trust is the firm belief in the reliability, honesty, integrity, ability, or strength of someone.

Creating a sense of trust is the most important factor when considering team member performance. Successful businesses are built on relationships, and the foundation of all relationships is trust. There may be times when some people may not see eye to eye.

However, if members treat each other with respect and kindness and can get their ideas across without feeling belittled or discriminated against, then trust can be built. Without trust, your ability to come to an agreement or build consensus will always be compromised.

What are the benefits of trust?

- Increases productivity and improves morale.

- Enables members to work more effectively as a team.

- Reduces the time needed to discuss key issues and make decisions (Appendix B).

- Facilitates cooperation and collaborative *problem-solving.

- Improves effectiveness and diminishes costs.

- Expands teamwork and sustainability.

Trust is the emotional component of companionship, friendship, love, agreement, relaxation, and comfort.

*To learn more about **Problem-Solving**, available at **Amazon.com,** see page 5.

Why are some bosses reluctant to delegate?

The main phobia bosses have about *delegating is losing control. I get it. However, the truth is that you never had control in the first place.

Control over other people is an illusion!

But, influence, through persuasion, is achievable.

The sooner you realize this fact, the quicker you'll be able to achieve order from chaos and let others do their job. The key to delegating is to do so gradually until you know who can move the work forward and who can't.

Here's a list showing levels of trust, starting with showing *very little trust* and ending with *complete trust*:

- Bring the facts to me for action (*little trust*).
- Develop alternatives, and I'll take action based on the facts.
- Be prepared to take action, but don't do anything until I say so.
- Tell me what you propose to do and when.
- Analyze the situation, take action, and tell me the results.
- Just go! Here's the situation; deal with it! (*complete trust*).

How do you build trust?

Do you know the most important components of building relationships? You shouldn't be surprised that it's trust. How much does your boss trust you? How much trust do you have in your team members?

Here are the important components of building trust:

- If others sense that you're AUTHENTIC, you're much more likely to be trusted.
- If others sense that your LOGIC is solid, you're far more likely to be trusted.
- If others sense your EMPATHY is sincere and directed at them, you're far more likely to be trusted.

When all three are present, you have their trust. But if any one of these three is missing or needs work, trust is in question.

*To learn more about **Delegating**, available at **Amazon.com,** see page 5.

How can you become more Authentic?

In human relations, your lack of authenticity is considered bad faith in dealing with other people. You'll tend to hold back who you really are for fear that someone might dislike you.

Authenticity is the degree to which your actions are congruent with your beliefs and desires, despite external pressures to conform.

You may even go so far as to be more like those with whom you work, hoping to fit in. Unfortunately, all this only makes you less likely to be trusted.

Pay less attention to what other people think about you and more attention to what you think about yourself. We all have an obligation to set and maintain the conditions that not only make it safe to be authentic but make it welcome. It's the key to achieving greater effectiveness.

How do you do it? You do it by being yourself and treating everyone with respect and kindness.

How can you enhance your Logic?

Logic is the study of correct reasoning, especially as it involves the drawing of inferences.

Logic has two gates you must pass through to be acceptable.

- First, is your logic must be rational, reasonable, and doable.

- Second, is your logic communicated in a way that's easily understood, straightforward, and supported with evidence.

How can you show Empathy?

Empathy is the capacity to understand or feel what another person is experiencing and the capacity to place oneself in another's position.

There are two levels of empathy:

- **Cognitive empathy** means that you're capable of *understanding* other people's thoughts and feelings.

- **Affective empathy,** in addition to *understanding*, means that you're capable of *feeling* other people's emotions and of sharing their grief, suffering, and joy.

In addition to creating trust, these three skills can help you build an emotional connection with others and truly relate to their feelings. Empathy can be learned to help bring you closer to having greater success in your relationships.

Are you a Micro-Manager?

Well, let's see. The opposite of effective delegation is micromanagement, where a boss gives too much input, direction, and review.

Micromanagement is a management style whereby the boss closely observes and controls the work of a Direct Report.

Micromanagement also includes the suppression of constructive criticism leads to job turnover. In micromanagement, the boss not only tells the Direct Report WHAT to do but dictates HOW to do it.

A frequent cause of micromanagement comes from the boss's doubt whether the Direct Report is competent enough to complete the project.

Effective delegation requires a well-defined objective, a clear vision of the constraints and dependencies, and effective oversight.

So, are you a micro-manager? Do you trust your Direct Reports? Would they agree? Any room for improvement?

32
BY BUILDING
CONSENSUS WITH A TEAM

"Unity is strength... when there is teamwork and collaboration,
wonderful things can be achieved."
- Mattie Stepanek

Do you know how to achieve agreement from all team members that they can support a proposal? Few people in the workforce today understand the meaning and value of collaborating to build consensus.

The process of building consensus starts with collaboration.

Collaboration is the process of working with others
to resolve a problem or achieve a goal.

Building consensus results from collaboration. Most people think that consensus means that everyone must like the proposal, the majority rules, or some other lame criteria - all of which are false.

Here's the truth!

Consensus is the desired end-product of
collaboration intended to achieve agreement from all
team members that they can support a proposal.

Support means that each member agrees that
the proposal will work and commits to doing all
they can to ensure its success.

If not, this is their chance to speak up! The process of building consensus gives every member the freedom to voice their agreements or disagreements before consensus is achieved. It's also intended to be inclusive, participatory, and cooperative, seeking opinions and input from all members. Consensus uses common agreement to resolve mutually exclusive positions. It's not the majority rules, nor a popularity contest. It doesn't care whose proposal is being considered or if any member likes or dislikes the proposal. It only asks each member if they can support the proposal. If not, a valid reason must be provided.

**VALID means that their reason must be either a
better proposal or a fact and not an opinion.**

Why is building consensus important?

To answer this question, I always ask,

What's the Greatest Hunger of the Human Heart?

What does every human being need to be fulfilled at work?

*The Greatest Hunger of the Human Heart
is to be NEEDED.*

To be needed means:

- To be seen means to be included and validated.
- To be heard means to be listened to, understood, and appreciated.
- To be valued means to be recognized for their contributions.
- To be treated with respect and kindness because they matter.

*The greatest hunger of the human heart is
to be seen, heard, valued, and treated with respect
and kindness because they matter.*

If team members aren't allowed to *"speak their piece,"* you're telling
them that they're not important and they don't matter. Not good! Do you
feel needed where you work? Do those who work with you feel
needed? Do you treat everyone with respect and kindness-no matter
what?

*Everyone needs to be engaged, involved, and have a say
concerning the things that affect their wellbeing.*

This is why consensus building is so powerful.

When's consensus needed?

Consensus is needed whenever you're trying to resolve a problem,
create a plan, or make any change that affects the team.

What are the benefits of building consensus?

- Consensus building improves the proposal by using the wisdom and knowledge of the team.

- It uncovers any Unintended Consequences and Second and Third-Order Effects that could slow or stop the proposal.

- It builds trust and commitment from the team by engaging them and using their input.

Building consensus is far more important than achieving it because, in the end, everyone may not agree to support the proposal, but at least they've been included in the process.

Failure to build consensus will erode teamwork, commitment and cause the failure to consistently produce excellent results. Building consensus sounds easy, but it's not. However, it's worth it because, without their involvement, they'll never be committed! And without their commitment, you'll never be able to consistently produce excellent results!

By building Consensus

Here are two methods of building consensus:

- **Staffing a Proposal.** This means circulating a proposal document through all team members to obtain their concurrence or non-concurrence with comments.

- **Conducting a Team Meeting.** This method works best when the proposal is an important decision that's time-sensitive, involves major funding, and affects the entire team.

If this is the case, here are the most important steps to build consensus.

Step 1. Discuss the proposal.

Gather the team, either at one location or on a phone or video conference and discuss the proposal.

- **If the proposal is a problem,** how was it discovered, how bad is it, and what're the risks if it continues unresolved? What's causing this problem? Is this the real problem or just a symptom? And how do we know for sure?

- **If the proposal is a goal,** why is it important? What's the intended benefit?

Step 2. Discuss the Solution.

If the solution is obvious, then work with the team to create the *Plan of Action* to implement the solution. If there could be several solutions, conduct a *Brainstorming Session* and select the best solution (Chapter 21).

Step 3. Anticipate the Consequences and Effects.

Once the solution has been identified, discuss the possible *Unintended Consequences* and *Second and Third-Order Effects* (Chapter 11).

Step 4. Eliminate all Unresolved Issues.

Discuss and identify all *Unresolved Issues* (any question, unknown, concern, shortfall, obstacle, or problem) that could slow or stop your progress (Chapter 10).

Step 5. Ask for Consensus.

Now, ask all team members if they can support the proposal. If not, why? Remember,

Support means that each member agrees that the proposal will work and commits to doing all they can to ensure its success.

If all members agree, ask them to create the *Plan of Action* to implement the proposed solution. If any member has a valid reason for non-support, continue to Step 6.

By resolving Reasons for Non-Support

At this point, only valid reasons should be considered. However, real-life doesn't work that way. Members will always have concerns and opinions, and they need to be heard. Here are the most important steps.

Step 6. Deal with their concerns.

If a member has a concern or opinion that's not a fact, this is when things get interesting.

- If their concern is that it's **too costly**, what does he mean? Too costly compared to what? How can the cost be reduced or offset? What's the contingency plan if it does cost more?

- If their concern is that it **will take much longer**, what's he basing this on? What's the downside if it does take longer? What's our Contingency Plan if it does?

- If their concern is that it's **too risky**, what does he mean? Can it be mitigated? Can a contingency plan be created just in case?

Step 7. Convert Reasons to Risks.

Before continuing, exchange the term *"Reason"* for *"Risk."* This will make this process much easier to understand. And for each risk, there are two critical things you must consider, probability and impact.

Step 8. What's the Probability?

How likely is this risk to happen (Chapter 12)? If the probability is *Low*, place the risk, *On-Hold*. This means that it's been noted and set aside temporarily. If the probability is *Medium* to *High*, or you're unsure, continue to the next step.

Step 9. What's the Impact?

What's the Impact or Effect on the proposal when this risk happens (Chapter 12)? If the Impact is *Minor,* place the risk *On-Hold.* If the Impact is *Moderate* to *Significant*, or you're unsure, continue to Step10.

Step 10. Can the Risk be Mitigated?

- If the risk can be mitigated, create a *Contingency Plan* (Chapter 15).

- If the risk can't be mitigated, you still have three options (Chapter 14).

Remember, you don't need a consensus before sending the proposal to your boss for approval. However, you'll need to include all reasons for non-support and let your boss decide. All members don't have to like the solution! They just need to be able to support it.

By Staffing a Proposal

Here's another method of building consensus without a meeting.

Staffing is the process of circulating a proposal document to all team members to obtain their concurrence or non-concurrence with comments in writing.

This method works best in situations where the proposal is routine and not time-sensitive. The proposal document could be a procedure, plan, question, or idea. Here are the four most important steps.

Step 1. Provide the proposal document to all members.

Ensure each team member receives a copy of the proposal document. Ask each member for their concurrence or non-concurrence with comments. And don't forget to provide a deadline.

Step 2. Resolve non-concur comments.

When member comments are returned to you, you may need to visit some members privately to better understand their comments and determine if adjusting your proposal could lead to their concurrence. Remember, concurrence means that each member agrees that:

The proposal will work and commits to doing all they can to ensure its success.

If not, a valid reason must be provided, which means their non-concur comments must be a better proposal or a fact and not an opinion.

Step 3. Make changes.

If you need to make changes, you'll need to send the revised proposal to all members again for another review. And for the second review, ensure you highlight any changes made from the first review.

Step 4. Obtain approval.

Note: You don't need the concurrence of all team members before sending your proposal to your boss for approval, but you'll need their reasons for non-concurrence. Remember, building consensus should never be done in a vacuum. You need the feedback to help you see beyond your blind spots.

33
BY SUPPORTING
TEAM GOALS

"The key to successful leadership today is influence, not authority."
- Ken Blanchard

Effective people know that to consistently produce excellent results, they must be actively involved in the daily process of supporting their team to achieve their goals.

By Motivating Team Members

Here are the most important things you can do to motivate team members.

- Partner with them to set their goals.

- Communicate Direction (Who, What, When, and Where).

- Provide structure, standards of behavior, and desired output and results.

- Provide challenging projects, access to information, and the authority to make *decisions to act on your behalf.

- Believe in them by displaying confidence, enthusiasm, and trust.

- Help them overcome obstacles and lighten their load.

- Provide feedback, keep them informed, and find out what's really going on.

- Show appreciation by thanking and praising.

- Provide recognition by awarding and promoting.

- Show encouragement by being visible, asking questions, paying attention, and showing interest.

- Be with them (your personal presence), look for the good, and be actively engaged.

- Encourage them to enhance their professional development (stretch goals).

*To learn more about *Decision-Making*, available at **Amazon.com,** see page 5.

- Communicate expectations, standards, and goals.
- Apply and share the eleven *Core Competencies of Effectiveness.*
- Anticipate and embrace change.
- Assess risk and exploit opportunities.
- Anticipate and quickly resolve problems.

By Inspiring Team Members

Here are the most important things you can do to inspire team members.

- Communicate the Purpose (Why) (a clear vision or direction of what's possible).
- Exemplify the highest moral, ethical, and professional behavior.
- Coach for peak performance (Chapter 26).
- Know the *Standards of Excellence* and be there to observe (Personal Presence).
- Think, speak, and act like a *Winner* (Chapter 30).
- Continually learn, apply, and share the eleven *Core Competencies of Effectiveness.*
- Facilitate collaborative Problem-Solving via collaboration and consensus-building (Chapter 32).

By showing your enthusiasm!

Effective people are passionate! They get fired up when needed. Be the cheerleader and champion the efforts of your team! Care deeply about what's important. Your lack of enthusiasm also speaks volumes. When you withhold your enthusiasm, you're telling those around you that the project is of lesser value. It's your enthusiasm that will attract the *"best and the brightest"* to work.

If you ever intend to show enthusiasm,

make sure you tell your face.

What attracts people will differ based on their needs, values, and circumstances. However, you can't generate enthusiasm in others if you're not enthused yourself.

By doing more than expected.

Do more than exist - Live!

Do more than touch - Feel!

Do more than look - Observe!

Do more than read - Absorb!

Do more than hear - Listen!

Do more than listen - Understand!

Do more than think - Ponder!

Do more than talk - Say Something!

Do more than belong - Participate!

Do more than care - Help!

Do more than believe - Practice!

Do more than be fair - Be kind!

Do more than forgive - Forget!

Do more than dream - Work!

- William Arthur Ward

Also:

Do more than Observe - ***Pay Attention!***
Do more than Be There - ***Get Involved!***
Do more than Get Involved – ***Show you Care!***
Do more than Show You Care – ***SERVE!*** (Chapter 37).

By acting confidently, even when you're not.

Confidence normally comes with time and experience. However, confidence is important because it enhances your credibility, believability, and trust. Their confidence in you reflects your self-confidence, certainty, composure, and outward calm through your display of emotions.

Careful! Sometimes confidence can be misinterpreted as arrogance. Make sure at least you know the difference. In your attempt to show confidence, the most important thing you can do is NOT to display a lack of confidence.

Here are the behaviors that indicate a lack of confidence.

- Complaining about your organization, boss, or job.

- Unwillingness to enforce organizational standards and any outward display of ignorance or apathy.

- Not responding to the needs of your members or becoming angry and agitated.

- Not asking for input from your members and the inability or unwillingness to make simple decisions.

Effective people complain up and praise down!

And let's not forget these behaviors that signal a lack of confidence:

Murmuring, evil speaking, hesitating, back-stepping, doubt, lack of faith, commitment, lack of self-esteem, attempts to evade, avoiding, procrastination, rationalizing, questioning, passive-aggressive behavior, blaming, and making excuses.

34
BY BUILDING
SOCIAL CAPITAL

"Leadership is the ability to establish standards and manage a creative climate where people are self-motivated toward the mastery of long-term constructive goals, in a participatory environment of mutual respect, compatible with personal values."
- Mike Vance

Superstars in business cause aggression, dysfunction, and waste. Often, the only way the most productive members can be successful is by suppressing the productivity of others. This is why *management by talent contest* has failed by routinely pitting one member or team against another.

And, to make things worse, business leaders have tried to motivate people with money, even though there's a vast amount of research showing that money erodes social connectedness. What makes one team more successful than another? The most successful teams have a high degree of social sensitivity or social connectedness to each other. And it all begins with the boss.

According to **Margaret Heffernan**, author of *Beyond Measure*, social capital relies on interdependency that builds trust and gives companies momentum and makes companies robust.

- **Soldiers and Marines have it.** They don't fight for money, medals, or country; they fight for their comrades.

- **The 2015 World Champion Kansas City Royals Baseball Team had it.** They don't win baseball games for money, glory, or Kansas City; they win for their teammates.

- **Firefighters have it.** They don't fight fires for money, glory, or their hometown; they fight to save innocent lives and the lives of their fellow Firefighters. "You go, I go!"

Social Capital compounds with time. Teams that work together longer get better because it takes time to develop the trust needed for real candor and openness. Time together, time to get to really know each other, is what builds trust.

"Leadership should be redefined as an activity in which conditions are created so everyone can do their most courageous thinking together."
- Margaret Heffernan

Conflict is frequent because candor is safe. And it's only through generous contribution, faith, and challenge that effective teams achieve their true potential.

As you treat members with respect and kindness, they'll do the same.

As the boss serves each team member, members begin to do the same (Chapter 37). They give equal time to each other so that no one voice dominates, and no one is left out. When team members are highly attuned and sensitive to each other, ideas can flow and grow. They don't get stuck. They don't waste energy *spinning-their-wheels.* Team members believe that everyone counts and that the team is far more important than anyone, especially the boss.

Members also believe that it's important that everyone makes it, and that they all rise or fall together.

There are no superstars-just solid contributors. Everyone gives the best they have-no matter what! What drives helpfulness is people getting to know each other. Teams that stop working and invest time in getting to know each other achieve real momentum. What motivates members are the bonds of loyalty and trust they develop between each other, much the same as in the US Military, the Kansas City Chiefs, and your local Firefighters.

Once you truly appreciate how social work is, a lot of good things start to happen. Social Capital replaces rivalry, and members begin to motivate each other by working and achieving together. This is why I created the eleven *Core Competencies of Effectiveness.*

Effective people are keenly aware that everybody has value. They invest in building *Social Capital* because they know it's the only way to liberate the energy, imagination, and momentum needed to consistently produce excellent results.

35
BY USING COMPETITION CAREFULLY

"Competition brings out the best in products and the worst in people."
- David Sarnoff

Have you ever played a game and observed the teamwork brought about by friendly competition?

- First, it's hard to find any athletic competition that's truly friendly.

- Second, this competition, in most cases, was focused more on member performance than team performance.

This is why some professional athletes get multi-million-dollar contracts, and others don't.

Here are three approaches to Member Competition:

- **Approach 1:** Compete by pitting one member against another. Here you'll have one *loser* and one *winner*. This form of competition can destroy cohesion and cooperation.

- **Approach 2:** Compete by pitting one member's results (monthly Sales $$) against every member on the team and publishing the results at the end of the month (rank-ordered from "most sales" at the top and "least sales" at the bottom). While this can be motivating for some, it could erode teamwork.

- **Approach 3:** Compete by pitting one member against a goal that he set for himself. Here the competition is against the standard, trying to beat their *last-personal-best*.

Here are two approaches to Team Competition:

- **Approach 1:** Compete by pitting one team against another. Here you still have one *winner* and one *loser*. However, playing against the best is the only way to elevate your game and improve. This may work great on the athletic field but probably not so well in business.

- **Approach 2:** Compete by pitting the entire team against goals they've set for themselves. This is the kind of competition you're looking for in a real team. This breeds cooperation and teamwork.

Which approach is Best?

It depends on your situation. Who produces the results: the team or member? Are you more concerned about the contributions of the team or a member?

- **Teamwork:** Since cooperation is what holds great teams together, have your team compete against a goal that they've set for themselves (collectively) and not against another team (so you don't have one *winner* and one *loser*).

- **Member:** Have the member compete against a goal that he has set for himself (his *last-personal-best*) and not against another member.

Note: To be effective, these goals, created by members and teams, must be measurable and contribute to their boss's goals. Also, if the team or member consistently exceeds their goals, they should be recognized.

36
BY CONDUCTING AN
AFTER-ACTION REVIEW

"We don't have a crisis of leadership in Washington.
We have a crisis of followership."
- Jonathan Rauch

How can you enhance your performance and the performance of your team? One way is to use *After-Action Reviews.*

An After-Action Review (AAR) is a professional discussion conducted after an activity, with all members present, seeking ways to consistently improve the way things are done.

AARs should be conducted both during (at the end of each day) and the day after an activity (project, objective, or goal) by measuring the difference between what was supposed to happen (the Plan) vs. what did happen (Behavior and Results).

AARs observe, measure, record, and assess an activity or process from start to finish to examine the results and the behavior of those involved.

The purpose of an AAR is to:

- Capture and share intuition by asking HOW and WHY questions.

- Attempt to discover WHY things happen and how to get better.

- Help members understand HOW and WHY decisions are made.

- Encourage members to become *self-correcting* and more *aware of how their behavior affects others (Appendix G).

- Capture *Lessons Learned* to integrate into future operations.

Here are the four most important steps to conducting an AAR:

Step 1. The Objective.

Before the activity (project, objective, or goal): What are we trying to achieve? What performance standards and results are desired? Who and what will be observed, and how will it be measured?

*To learn more about *Awareness*, available at **Amazon.com,** see page 5.

Step 2. The Results and Behavior.

During the activity: What happened? What was observed and measured? What are the facts?

Step 3. The Assessment.

After the activity: Did things go as expected? Were there any surprises? If the result wasn't what we expected, what should be started, stopped, or changed to achieve a better result? WHY and HOW did we do what we did?

Step 4. The Lessons Learned.

What did we learn that can help us do better next time?

By using Informal After-Action Reviews

Let's assume that you're the Project Manager for a four-day Trade Show and you have three team members.

The week before the show, you and your boss sat down to discuss the plan and its objective. Why are we attending this show? What's the ideal outcome you'd like to see? How will this outcome be measured? After finishing with your boss, you met with your team and briefed them on the plan. Fast forward to the end of the first day of the show. You assembled your team and asked, what did we learn today that can make us better tomorrow?

One team member said it would have been nice to have some bottled water in our booth. A second member said, we also need a lunch schedule, so everyone has a chance to eat. Also, we're running low on our advertising brochures. You then asked one team member to provide bottled water in the booth every day. Then you asked another member to set up a lunch schedule for each day. And finally, you called your boss and asked him to overnight a bunch of advertising brochures. You also conducted an informal review at the end of each day with the goal of continuous improvement.

The day after the trade show, you gathered your team together and asked if we accomplished our goal? Did everything go as planned? Were there any surprises? What did we learn that could make the next Trade Show better? You then added all comments to your After-Action Report so next year's Trade Show can be even better. How hard was that?

37
BY SERVING
THE TEAM

"The first responsibility of a leader is to define reality.
The last is to say thank you.
In between, the leader is a servant."
- Max DePree.

Effective bosses strengthen their credibility by serving those that help them consistently produce excellent results.

Serving means taking care of others.

Serving is simple but not easy because to do it right demands your dedication, sacrifice, humility, discipline, long-term commitment, and willingness to change. There are only two ways of serving anyone: reducing or eliminating their pain or increasing their pleasure. It's true, think about it.

Everyone's behavior is driven by either reducing or eliminating their pain or increasing pleasure.

What pleasures do humans seek?

Love, recognition, power, encouragement, reward, success, money, food, meaningful work, comfort, promotions, freedom, convenience, free time, money, leisure, caring, health, and anything else could keep them in their Comfort Zone (Chapter 13).

What pains do humans avoid?

Failure, shame, rejection, loneliness, anguish, grief, disappointment, betrayal, death, death of a loved one, suffering, divorce, bankruptcy, boring and repetitive work, do-overs, embarrassment, mistakes, frustration, setbacks, waiting on others, wasting their time, indecision, "unacceptable" behavior, conflict, struggle, uncertainty, and anything that could cause physical or mental discomfort or could take them out of their Comfort Zone.

Ultimately, it's the team members who determine their boss's level of effectiveness and success.

Bosses need willing and capable *followers. There's little more frustrating than having good members leave. Since they can leave you at any time, what do you offer them to stay and give their best effort every day?

What's Serving?

Serving is doing what needs to be done, to the best of your ability, without being told to do so, when no one is watching, and without expecting any recognition.

These five distinct components of serving are critical. If any are missing, you're not serving. So, for example, if you're expecting recognition in return, you're working, not serving.

Service must be selfless - done for the benefit of others.

What are the five most important components of serving?

- **Doing what needs to be done:** This requires that you take the action necessary to help others in some meaningful way.

- **To the best of your ability:** Why would you bother doing anything if it wasn't your best effort?

- **Without being told to do so:** Being told to do so is doing work, not service. What if no one is around to tell you what to do?

- **When no one's watching:** Are you doing this to get the praise of others? If so, that's not service because you're doing it for yourself.

- **Without expecting any recognition:** If you are doing it to receive recognition for yourself, you're not serving others, and others can see that. If what you're doing is for the betterment of others, you're serving. It's your intent that counts.

*To learn more about **Followership**, available at **Amazon.com,** see page 5.

Now what? My advice: Do more than expected,
Follow-through, and repeat often!

Only by truly serving others can you ever expect to gain the degree of credibility you'll need to influence the actions of others.

I'm often asked,

How do you know what NEEDS to be done?

I always answer by asking this question,

What did **Mother Teresa** do when she started the Missionaries of Charity?

How did she know what needed to be done? In 1950, she started with nothing but a burning desire and God's help. Soon she had 13 Sisters serving with her in the slums of Calcutta, making sure no one died abandoned and alone.

47 years later, in 1997, the Missionaries of Charity had grown to over 4000 sisters serving worldwide. She just showed up with a helpful heart, ready to get involved, and the work presented itself.

The message here is Simple but Powerful:
To find out what needs to be done, show up with
a helpful heart, ready to get involved, and
the work will present itself.

What are the three most important requirements?

- *To show up: Means being there! Never underestimate the power of your presence.*

- **With a helpful heart:** Means asking, *"How can I help? What do you need?"* Then, ask yourself, *"Would you be willing to do what they do under the same conditions?"*

- **Ready to get involved:** Means *committing to purpose* (Chapter 28) and ready to contribute in some meaningful way. This can only be achieved by knowing their names, the culture, values, rules, policies, standards, ethics, expectations, equipment, property, chain of authority, limitations, capabilities, and do's and don'ts, just to mention a few.

If you don't have all three, work hard until you do. Without having all three, you won't be able to see what you need to see, to feel what you need to feel, and to act the way you need to act - to truly serve others (Chapter 37).

What matters most in life?

It's taken me a lifetime to finally answer this question for myself.

- **What matters MOST** in my life is love, faith, duty, family, friends, relationships, serving others, contributions, and preparing for my life after death.

- What matters least in my life is money, power, fame, prestige, expensive toys, the trappings of wealth, distractions, and the sham and glitter of this world.

Note: What matters most in your life? How much time do you spend there? If I followed you for a day, would I find you spending most of your time doing the things that matter most?

38

BY PROTECTING
THE TEAM

*"Man becomes great exactly in the degree in which
he works for the welfare of his fellow-men."
- Mahatma Gandhi*

Effective people know how important it is to protect the *Health and Welfare* of their team because they know what happens if they don't. But what does that mean?

**Protecting the Health and Welfare of your team
means maintaining the stability, harmony, integrity,
cohesion and productivity of the team.**

This means that any behavior that threatens the team's stability, harmony, integrity, or cohesiveness is unacceptable. Any person, or persons, who violate this standard or exhibit any hostility or dissension must be released for the team's good.

How do you know what's most important?

No one is more important than the team that produces the results. No one is safe from being let go. Why is that? Well, consider this, what happens to unsuccessful NFL Football Coaches near the end of every season? They get fired!

It's not Personal; it's Business!

If you can't produce the desired result, your boss will be looking for someone who can. He has no choice unless he wants his position to be in question. Do your results contribute to your boss's goals? If you and your team consistently produce excellent results that contribute to your boss's goals, you're in good shape. If not, you need to get there or seek work elsewhere. This is the harsh reality of the *world of work*.

Also, if someone's results or behavior are disruptive to the team, *corrective action* must be taken quickly and privately - for the team's good.

Other team members are watching and expecting you to consistently maintain the standards and to hold all members accountable for their performance. If you don't, you'll quickly lose credibility with your team and your boss.

By protecting the Health and Welfare of the Team

Effective bosses protect their team by:

- **Maintaining high standards of performance by:**
  - ✓ Giving feedback and coaching (praising, appreciating, recognizing, and rewarding).
  - ✓ Correcting (rework and retraining).
  - ✓ Punishing (warnings, reprimands, probation, termination, and even legal action).
  - ✓ Maintaining a safe, secure, inclusive, and worry-free environment.

- **Doing all they can to keep their members healthy by:**
  - ✓ Getting a Flu shot and encourage your members to do the same.
  - ✓ Ensuring members stay home if sick (keep them healthy).
  - ✓ Ensuring members take time off for lunch, holidays, and vacation.
  - ✓ Encouraging members to wash their hands, use hand sanitizers, and avoid touching doorknobs.

- **Doing your Duty:**

The hardest part of doing your duty will come when you make corrections, maintain standards, assess behavior and results, discipline or release members, and tell your boss what he doesn't want to hear, like the Truth.

39
BY CREATING A
PHILOSOPHY OF SERVING

Do you have a *Philosophy of Serving?*

A Philosophy of Serving is a written document explaining how you intend to treat your team members when placed in a position of authority.

Horace Greely had it right when he said:

> *"Fame is a vapor, popularity an accident, riches take wings. Only one thing endures, and that is character."*

Team members want to know how you're going to lead them. Don't make them guess on rumors, past accomplishments, or the opinions and stories of others. Come out and tell them in the first few days by giving them a copy of your *Philosophy of Service.* Then back it up by what you do because they won't be watching your lips; they'll be watching your feet.

How do you intend to add value to their lives? It should also reflect how you intend to apply the *11 Core Competencies of Effectiveness.* What are the things you want your members to focus on during your tenure? It could include things like initiative, problem resolution, or customer care.

Whatever it is, one way to reinforce that desired behavior is through a written *Philosophy of Serving.* It's a window into your character, revealing how you intend to treat others.

Character is the foundation of your Effectiveness.

Let's see if you can create a *Philosophy of Service* that inspires you and those in your charge and will become your compass to guide you – especially during difficult times.

To create your *Philosophy of Serving,* answer these questions.

- What do you expect from your team?

- What should they expect from you?

- What's important to you?

- How do you feel about duty and service?

- How do you feel about your team members?

- How do you personally define service?

- What have been some of the defining experiences in your life?

- What are the key lessons of service you'd like to teach others?

- What impact do you want to make in the world?

- What do you stand for? What will you not stand for?

- What's your purpose?

- What are your fundamental values, beliefs, and principles that guide your service to others?

- What behavior is unacceptable?

Here's an example of a *Philosophy of Service*:

"My Philosophy of Service is embodied by my personal belief that people are honest, decent, and good, and at the end of the day, they truly want to do the right thing. My entire life has been dedicated to helping others achieve goals they previously thought were impossible.

I believe that our human potential is unlimited, and it's only in our moments of testing ourselves (or being tested by life) that we truly see what we can achieve. I believe in you and what you can achieve.

I believe that small, highly trained, cross-functional teams are what drive success at any level. Teams are quick to see changes and to act decisively to do the right things. I know that fatigue, negative emotions, miscommunication, animosity, ignorance, apathy, and complacency are the enemy of everything we do as a team.

Expect that I will do all I can to combat these from occurring, and I expect my managers to do the same.

You can expect that I will:

- *Care about you and your family.*

- *Treat you with respect and kindness.*

- *Listen carefully and respectfully to what you say.*

- *Support you in achieving your goals and your desire to be the best.*

- *Be thoughtful and responsive to your needs and concerns.*

I expect that you will:

- *Do all you can to support your boss.*

- *Do your best every day and seek ways to improve what you do.*

- *Accept accountability for your actions and the consequences.*

- *Improve your skills through further education and training.*

- *Do everything you can to support your fellow team members.*

- *Be a Team Player: Cooperate, Coordinate, and Collaborate.*

- *Reveal problems and be honest in your dealings with others.*

- *Treat everyone with respect and kindness.*

- *Play by the rules, unless you have a good reason for not doing so.*

- *Not engage in negative speaking unless it's behind closed doors in my office.*

For my managers, once you're trained, I expect you to take the initiative; be proactive. I'm a strong believer in personal responsibility. Errors of commission will be corrected, but errors of omission are far more serious. Successful job performance entails accepting the risk of being corrected for errors and undo or redo some work. Exercising initiative is a requirement for successful service here.

I look forward to the privilege of serving you to the best of my ability."

Could you get by without a *Philosophy of Serving*? Sure. But when team members know upfront who you are and how you intend to treat them, they won't have to figure it out for themselves. More importantly, they can now begin the process of trusting you.

It's another great tool to have in your *Effectiveness Toolbox*. Let it guide and inspire you to make a difference for those you serve.

This page is intentionally left blank.

APPENDIX A:
DEMONSTRATE
GOOD JUDGMENT

"Experience is simply the name we give our mistakes."
- Oscar Wilde

In your attempt to save time, do you rush and make snap decisions without considering the consequences?

Good judgment is your ability to bring together reason and wisdom to analyze a situation, explore your options, select a course of action, and take action.

Good judgment isn't about being smart or about making good decisions (Appendix B).

The essence of good judgment is about

learning from past mistakes.

It's about using your *Assessment Systems* (Appendix C) to ensure you don't repeat the same mistakes and increase the probability of success of your next attempt.

Judgment is less about getting it right and more

about what it takes to learn what went wrong.

Some of your decisions will result in *Unintended Consequences* (Appendix F). To add to this uncertainty, you'll soon discover that your decisions aren't always about what's good or bad. Often, they're about choosing between good, better, and best. All decisions have consequences, which you won't see in advance. But experience teaches that they'll come due someday.

Where do good decisions come from?

Good decisions don't happen by accident.

- Good decisions come from good judgment.
- Good judgment comes from failure (Appendix C).
- Failure comes from mistakes.

- Mistakes come from bad decisions.

- Bad decisions come from bad judgment.

- Bad judgment comes from a lack of experience.

- Lack of experience comes from:
  - ✓ Having little time invested in the job.
  - ✓ Not learning from your mistakes.
  - ✓ Not learning from the mistakes of others.
  - ✓ Making quick decisions when you have more time.
  - ✓ A failure to venture outside your comfort zone.

Mistakes, as long as you learn from them, are the building blocks of greatness.

How can you learn from the mistakes of others?

Learning from the mistakes of others only happens if you're paying attention. The truth is that anyone can cut their learning curve and gain years of valuable experience by using this simple principle:

There are only two ways to learn anything in life, either by trial and error or by modeling the best practices.

While it's important to learn from your mistakes, it's a lot easier to learn from the mistakes of others.

How can Modeling help you?

Experience is the toughest teacher because it gives the test first and the knowledge second.

Modeling a better teacher because it gives you the knowledge, so you're better prepared for the test.

Modeling is the process of learning from those who've already achieved success.

It also means learning by copying the behavior of those who've already experienced the mistakes and failures on their journey to success (Appendix C). You can avoid the same mistakes and failures by learning, applying, and sharing what you'll learn here.

B
KNOW WHEN TO
ACT, WAIT OR WALK AWAY

"You got to know when to hold 'em. Know when to fold 'em.
Know when to walk away and know when to run."
- Kenny Rogers, The Gambler.

When faced with a problem, how do you know what to do? For every problem you'll face, you'll normally have three choices of how to respond:

You can act, wait, or walk away.

When faced with a problem, can't you just do nothing? Sure. Think about it. You have this option every time you're faced with a problem. Do some problems sometimes correct themselves by doing nothing? Yes. Do some problems get worse by taking action rather than doing nothing? You bet!

Remember, doing nothing is deciding by default.

Are there some problems that are better left alone? Sure. Just ask any Fire-fighter. Most of the time, all they can do is contain the fire and just let it burn itself out; let it *burn-to-the-ground*. If you feel this is your best choice, among all the choices you have at the time, then do nothing – let it *burn-to-the-ground*.

However, doing nothing and waiting
are two different options.

When faced with any problem, use these steps to guide your response.

Step 1: Should I Act NOW?

Before deciding, answer these questions?

- Can this problem be resolved by calling 911? If Yes, call!

- Will acting now save lives or avoid further damage?

  ✓ If Yes, take *Immediate Action* (Appendix D).

  ✓ If No to both questions, continue to Step 2.

Step 2: Is this my problem?

Is this my problem or someone else's?

- Who has the most to gain or lose from its resolution?
- Who's affected by this problem?

If this problem isn't your problem, why are you trying to solve it? Just report it to your boss and walk away. If this is your problem, continue to the next step.

Step 3: Should I act now or wait?

How urgent is this problem?

- How important or urgent is this problem and why?
- What must happen before I'm forced to act?
- What are the consequences if this problem remains unresolved?
- What's the downside of waiting?

How much time do I have?

- How long do I have before this problem becomes a crisis?
- How long do I have before I'm forced to act?
- When's it too late to act?

Based on your answers to the above questions, use the *Decision Support Template* below to guide your decision.

Here's an example of a *Decision Support Template*: Time vs. Urgency.

Decision Support Matrix		Time to Decide?	
		Little Time	Enough Time
Urgency?	Urgent	1	2
	Not Urgent	3	4

Here's what the numbers mean:

1. If this problem is urgent and you have little time to decide, take *Immediate Action* (Appendix D) and develop a mental *Plan of Action* before acting (Appendix E). See CONPLAN 1.

2. If this problem is urgent and you have enough time, take Step 4. Prepare to act after completing your *Plan of Action*. Keep your boss informed. See CONPLAN 2.

3. If this problem isn't urgent and you have little time to decide, wait, continue to monitor the situation, create your *Plan of Action*, and keep your boss informed. See CONPLAN 3.

4. If this problem isn't urgent and you have enough time to act, continue to monitor the situation, create your *Plan of Action*, and update your boss. See CONPLAN 4.

Also, document what happened, when, and who took action to resolve the problem for investigative or legal purposes later.

Step 4: Create your Plan of Action.

See Appendix E.

Note: You're responsible for anticipating the consequences and effects (Appendix F) of your work BEFORE deciding.

Other Things to Consider

When's the best time to decide?

> **"The key is not to make quick decisions,**
> **but to make timely decisions."**
> **- Colin Powell**

Do you have to make the decision right now? This classic answer is usually, No! This is rarely necessary. Resist the impulse of making a snap decision when there's no need to do so. Normally, you'll have sufficient time to decide.

A good rule of thumb is to decide after acquiring **40-70%** of the information you need. Mistakes, as long as you learn from them, are the building blocks of greatness. If it turns out bad, adjust, and remember what you've learned for next time.

Who's the Best Person to decide?

First, the boss decides, followers recommend! Or, at least, the boss should take responsibility and ownership of his team's decisions, especially if it turns out bad. Ask members for their input before you decide. Also, if the decision affects everyone in your team, why can't all members be given a chance to concur or non-concur with reasons (Chapter 32)?

Does the Best Decision always produce the Best Outcome?

There's a big difference between your decision and the result or outcome of your decision. You could be the most experienced decision-maker on the planet, and you could make the best decision, but there's no guarantee that your problem will be resolved or the best outcome will be achieved. You can actually make a good decision, and the results could still be bad. The situation and facts available when you first decided could (and probably will) change over time. What was good today could turn out to be bad tomorrow.

Do you need your Boss's Approval?

Have you ever been in a situation where you were waiting for your boss's approval? Why are you asking for approval if the problem is internal, doesn't require additional resources you don't have, and isn't in conflict with any internal standards? That's what your boss is paying you to do. But do let him know.

Sometimes it's easier to ask forgiveness than permission.

Or, if you're in doubt, tell your boss when you'll be making your decision (like the end of the week), and if you don't hear from him before that time, you'll be moving forward. Don't forget to assess the consequences and effects of your actions.

What if a Direct Reports recommends a change?

One of the best bosses I ever worked with once said,

> **"If I can't give you a good reason not to make the change; I'll approve it."**

Yes, they still had to create a *Decision Paper*, build consensus with the team (Chapter 32), and present it to the team for a final discussion before approval. This gave the team the freedom they needed to make things better.

C
LEARN FROM
MISTAKES AND FAILURE

Will you make mistakes and have failures in your lifetime? You bet lots of them. But that's how we all learn. So, how can you learn from mistakes and failure? Effective people know that the only thing that matters is what you learn for the next time.

What's Failure?

The dictionary defines failure as:

> *"The state or condition of not meeting a desirable or intended goal and may be viewed as the opposite of success."*

Failure is a relative term. It's viewed differently depending on your situation and who's doing the viewing. For example, failure to a baseball player may be striking out, but failure to his coach might be losing the game. In the Business World, your goals will come from your boss. Did you accomplish the goals you were assigned? Did you achieve the result you wanted? If not, why?

The only important question is, what did you learn that can make you better next time? I used to think that there was no such thing as failure (it didn't exist) as long as you never gave up. But this is only partially true and sends the wrong message. You'll experience mistakes and failures in your life. The trick is not to let them define you.

Instead, let them Refine you and make you stronger!

The past doesn't equal the future. Learn what you need to learn and move on!

What's the difference between a failure and an unsuccessful attempt?

- **Failure** needs a substantial loss (like money, time, or reputation).

- **An Unsuccessful Attempt** means that your last attempt did not achieve the desired result.

However, if you can make another attempt, did you learn why the last attempt was unsuccessful? Do you know what changes need to be made for your next attempt to be successful?

The example most often used comes from the story of **Thomas Edison** and his 10,000 attempts to create the incandescent light bulb. Just remember, *Edison* could make as many attempts as he needed until he was successful because he wasn't paying for each attempt. His investors were paying the bills. Most people don't have that luxury.

Failure only exists if there's a loss.
The bigger the loss, the bigger the failure.

What's Failure in the Real World?

There are two types of failure which are commonly misunderstood:

- **Personal failure:** This is an unsuccessful attempt at accomplishing your personal goal and includes a:
  - ✓ **Failure to try.** This means never setting goals or never attempting to accomplish anything.
  - ✓ **Failure to keep trying.** This means that after an unsuccessful initial attempt, you failed to learn from your mistakes, make the changes needed, find a different way to get there, or make another attempt.
  - ✓ **Substantial Loss.** This is a loss of your wealth, relationships, health, character, or reputation.
- **Company failure:** This is a failure to accomplish an assigned goal, resulting in losing anything your boss couldn't afford to lose.

Let's examine what should happen BEFORE you attempt to accomplish any goal.

Step 1. What's the Risk?

Conduct a *Risk Assessment* to look for all the things that could reasonably go wrong during your attempt. Collaborate to assess all your safety, security, financial, and operational risk and how they can be mitigated.

Step 2. How many attempts?

If you know you'll only get one attempt, make it count! If you know you'll get as many attempts as you need, then the only risk is the cost of each additional attempt. Remember **Edison**?

Step 3. What's the cost?

- **Cost:** What will it cost to make this attempt (how much time, money, or effort will it take)?

- **Opportunity Costs:** What are you losing by not using other alternatives?

Step 4. What if you're wrong?

Can everyone live with an unsuccessful attempt?

Step 5. What are the benefits?

What benefits will you receive if your attempt is successful?

Step 6. Is the benefit worth the cost?

- **If Yes**: Continue to create your *Plan of Action* (Appendix E).

- **If No or Unsure:** Work hard to mitigate your Risk. Then, conduct another Cost/Benefit Analysis.

Step 7. What's your Assessment System?

An *Assessment System* is a series of procedures designed to measure the most critical parameters of your attempt to determine what went wrong, right, and why? How will the attempt be measured? How do you know when it's time to *pull-the-plug?*

An Assessment System is a combination of targeted, proactive procedures designed to identify problems before they occur and resolve problems once identified.

This system is called CAPA (Corrective Actions, Preventive Actions) and should be part of your overall Quality Management System (QMS) and includes procedures to prevent problems (PA) and procedures to correct problems (CA) once identified.

After the Attempt

Let's examine what should happen AFTER your attempt.

Step 8. Was the attempt a complete success?

- **If Yes:** Congrats! What's next?
- **If No:** If your attempt was unsuccessful, was there a loss?
  - ✓ If there was NO loss, what did you learn, and what changes need to be made? Never give up! Just find another way to get there.
  - ✓ If there was a loss, now you have a real failure. The greater the loss, the greater the failure.

Step 9. What did you learn from your Assessment System?

- What went wrong, right, and why?
- What needs to change to make your next attempt a success?
- How will you know when it's time to *pull-the-plug*?

The lesson may have been painful, but don't throw the learning away. Mistakes and failures can be your best teacher, but only if you remember the lesson. Now what? Well, that depends on you!

Is Failure Fatal?

"Failure is not fatal, but failure to change might be."
- John Wooden

Assuming your attempt resulted in a loss, it's not the end of your life or your career. And, sometimes, getting close is good enough. Assess what happened, what you learned, and get *back-in-the-game!*

Never give up! Just find another way to get there.

D
TAKE
IMMEDIATE ACTION

When bad things happen, what do you usually do? Don't just sit there, do something! But what?

Immediate Action is a proactive eight-step process used to react to any bad situation that could cause a work stoppage, property damage, a security breach, or physical injury.

Let's drill down on the eight steps of the *Immediate Action* process.

Step 1. Assess the Situation.

Either be *on-the-scene* or in communication with someone on the ground. Assess the situation based on the facts.

Step 2. Notify Emergency Services and your boss.

If needed, call 911, and call your boss to tell him what you know.

Step 3. Consider your Options.

Look around. What's available for you to use? What should be done to stabilize the situation? What are your options? If time permits, collaborate with others.

Step 4. Select the Best Option.

Select the best option, and if time permits, achieve consensus with those around you.

Step 5. Create a Plan of Action.

Create a quick mental *Plan of Action*. What's the first step? What's the second, and so forth?

Step 6. Take Decisive Action.

Using what's available, *take-charge*, and give new instructions to others. Supervise their actions.

Step 7. Reassess the Situation.

What, if anything, has changed? Did the situation stabilize, or was the problem resolved? If Yes, move to Step 8. If NO, repeat this process.

Step 8. Call your boss.

Keep your boss informed. Explain what happened, what caused it, and what you recommend be done to ensure this never happens again. Sounds pretty easy, right? Well, let's see how it's done in the real world.

True Story

At 9 AM, two days before his company's annual Team Building Session, Bob, the Project Manager, conducted his final site inspection of the resort and was astonished by what he saw. He tried to pull into the resort, but it was blocked by construction vehicles tearing up the parking lot. This was a disaster for Bob because he had 50 Senior Executives flying in from all over the country for this session. Fortunately, Bob knew how to take Immediate Action.

Step 1. Assess the Situation.

Bob didn't panic. He assessed the situation, took photos with his cell phone, spoke with the resort manager, and learned that a major water main had broken, which meant that the resort had no water. Bob also talked to the on-site construction manager and learned that the water main could not be repaired for another week.

Step 2. Call Emergency Services and your boss.

At 9:30 AM: Since there was no need to call 911, Bob called his boss and appraised him of the situation.

Step 3. Consider your options.

At 10 AM, Bob called a meeting of all Key Players at company headquarters to collaborate to find the best solution. Bob asked one Key Player to find another venue that could accommodate 50 people. By 11 AM, a new venue had been found, but it was 27 miles from the airport. One problem was solved, but it created another. How will all attendees get from the airport to the resort? Someone asked, can't they just catch a cab or just rent a car at the airport? For 50 people to catch a cab or rent a car would be way too expensive.

Step 4. Select the best option.

Then someone suggested that they rent a fleet of shuttle vehicles with drivers to transport all attendees from the airport to the resort and back. They all agreed that this was the best solution.

Step 5. Create a Plan of Action.

Together they created a Plan of Action to use shuttle vehicles to accomplish the objective.

Step 6. Take Decisive Action.

Bob issued new instructions to all Key Players and supervised their actions. He assigned one Key Player to contact all attendees to let them know what happened and look for company signs at the airport directing them to shuttle vehicles rather than taking a cab or renting a vehicle. Bob also asked a second Key Player to identify and contract a shuttle company to transport all attendees. He asked everyone to meet again at 5 PM to share the status of their new assignments.

Step 7. Reassess the Situation.

At 5 PM that afternoon, Bob met with all Key Players to ensure everything was ready to move forward with a fleet of shuttle vehicles.

Step 8. Report to your boss.

At 6 PM, Bob called his boss and informed him that the problem was resolved by selecting a new site and renting a fleet of shuttle vans to drive all attendees from the airport to the hotel and back. There was no reason to recommend what needed to be done to ensure this didn't happen again. The Team Building Session went on without any further problems and turned out to be a great success.

Bob looked defeat in the eye and refused to give up,

"Snatching Victory from the Jaws of Defeat."

And you can do the same!

This page is intentionally left blank.

E
CREATE
A PLAN OF ACTION

Here's a great checklist to use when creating your next *Plan of Action*.

OBJECTIVE (Who, What, When, Where, and Why?)

- What's my access to sources of info, and who's this project for?
- Where and Why is this project being conducted?
- How important is this project, and to whom is it important?
- How will success be measured, and who will measure it?
- What's the requirement, scope, and complexity of work?
- What's the limit of my authority (decisions, delegate, spend $, hire, and fire)?
- Does someone with authority approve this?
- When does this project start and end?
- What's the most important task for this project to be a success?
- Who has done this task before, and what were their problems, consequences, and effects?
- What must be ordered or started now?

METHODS (How)

- How should we do it? What are all our options, which is best?
- What needs to happen during the four phases of this project?
- What're all the tasks involved, and who are responsible for performing each task (Key Player)?
- What must be done before, during, and after the project?
- What specific instructions do we have for those delegated a task?
- How many are expected to attend or are affected by this?
- What're our restrictions (can't do) and imperatives (must do)?

- Who has done this or a similar type of project before?

- How will this project be advertised or promoted?

- What are my responsibilities, expectations, duties, constraints, authority, and standards?

- Who're the most important people to talk to right now?

- What're the consequences if this turns out unsuccessful?

TIMETABLE

- Planning backward from today, when are the *Planning, Preparing, Executing, and Assessment Phases?

- When's the *Backbriefing?*

- What's the *Project Update Briefing* schedule?

- Which *Preventive Actions* must be done during each phase (Appendix E)?

- How long will each task take, and what's the best sequence of these tasks and *Preventive Actions?*

- Which tasks can't start or finish without another task starting or finishing? (Dependent tasks)

- Which task needs to be started right now?

- What's the detailed schedule, program, and calendar?

- When's the rehearsal, and what will be rehearsed?

- What else is going on in the company or **community at the same time? What happened last year at this time?

*To learn more about *Planning*, available at **Amazon.com,** see page 5.

**Do you really want your project to go on at the same time as Spring Break, the Superbowl, or a Presidential Election Voting Day?

RESOURCES

- What resources are most important for the success of this project?

- How much of each resource is needed, when, and where?

- Who's responsible (Key Player) for providing these resources?

- When's the latest time we need these resources delivered?

- Who's paying for this, and what must be ordered now?

- What skills, attitudes, or knowledge are needed, and who has the skills we need?

- Any special needs for safety, security, sanitation, disabilities?

- What're our *Shortfalls* (anything you need to complete a project that you don't have)?

- How much money can we spend? What's our Budget?

UNRESOLVED ISSUES

- What do we need to know but don't?

- What do we know for sure, but the answer is unsatisfactory or unacceptable?

- What are our shortfalls, which are things we need but don't have?

- What are all the *Unresolved Issues* (questions, unknowns, concerns, shortfalls, obstacles, or problems) that could slow or stop your progress (Appendix E)?

Who has done this type of work before, and what were their problems, consequences, and effects (Appendix F)?

RISK

- **Physical: (Injury, Illness, or Death)**

  - ✓ Have we inspected the site for anything that could cause injury, illness, accident, or death?

  - ✓ Have we inspected for sanitation and access for those with disabilities?

- **Security: (Cyber and Physical)**
  - ✓ For Cybersecurity: What could cause a data breach, loss of personal info or intellectual property, or a disruption of services?
  - ✓ For Physical Security: What could cause unauthorized access leading to theft, fraud, waste, abuse, or property damage?
- **Financial:**
  - ✓ What could cause financial loss or property damage?
  - ✓ What insurance do we need, and is it in-force?
- **Operational:**
  - ✓ What's the *Impact and Probability* when these risks occur?
  - ✓ How can these risks be mitigated?
  - ✓ What's your *Contingency Plan* for when they do?
  - ✓ What assumptions are needed to move the work forward)?
  - ✓ What **Preventive Actions* did you add to your POA?
  - ✓ Have you ***Staffed* your POA with the team?
  - ✓ What are you forgetting to do?

---

*Impact** means how <u>serious</u> this risk will affect the project, and Probability means how <u>likely</u> this risk will happen?

Preventive Actions are all the things you should be doing 30, 60, or 90 days before any project to uncover all your Pre-Problems. Pre-Problems are mistakes, defects, shortfalls, omissions, errors, or anything else that could slow or stop your work.

***Staffing** is the process of circulating a proposal document to all team members to obtain their concurrence or non-concurrence with written comments (Chapter 32).

F
ANTICIPATE
CONSEQUENCES AND EFFECTS

Do you know how to anticipate and mitigate anything that could produce unexpected outcomes, causing delays or stoppage to your project?

By anticipating Unintended Consequences

Unintended Consequences are outcomes that aren't the outcomes expected from your project.

Unintended Consequences fall into three categories:

- **A positive**, unexpected benefit, which is usually referred to as serendipity or a windfall.

- **A negative**, unexpected problem like irrigation providing water for agriculture could also lead to cholera.

- The consequence of **what others might say or do** is referred to as backlash, fallout, or blowback.

Here's an example of a negative Unintended Consequence.

Can you tell what's wrong with this picture? Hint: Does Starbucks really suck?

Answer: The painters applied the Starbucks advertising on a delivery van with the doors closed.

Unfortunately, they failed to consider the unintended consequences of what the van would look like when the side door was open. This is *Murphy's Law* at its best!

By anticipating Second and Third-Order Effects

Be sensitive to how your work affects others.

Second and Third-Order Effects focus on how your work will affect others at different levels in your company.

Different levels mean how your work will affect others in your unit, department, company, and suppliers. *Second and Third-Order Effects* may also identify new resource requirements and cause changes to structures and procedures.

For example, if you decide to change a supplier, the effects could be extensive.

- *Second-Order Effects* could require new ordering procedures to be created, which could cause delays.

- *Third-Order Effects* could require others to be retrained on new ordering procedures and software.

To anticipate *Second and Third-Order Effects* keep asking.

Now, what? What's next? What're we forgetting? And what could happen or what might we need to do in 30, 60, or 90 days?

G
ASSESS YOUR
ACCOUNTABILITY

Do you know what to do when your boss finds something wrong with your work?

Accountability is the acceptance of responsibility for your actions and in-actions and the obligation to report, explain, and be answerable for any adverse consequences.

Accountability is often confused with responsibility. They're related but different. *Accountability* is normally not a problem - until something goes wrong.

For example, if something goes wrong within your area of responsibility, you'll get the chance to explain what happened to your boss, and maybe his boss. Sometimes, depending on the severity of the problem, your boss won't be happy with you and may treat you badly.

Most people don't understand that, yes, responsibility and *accountability* go together; they're part of the same iceberg.

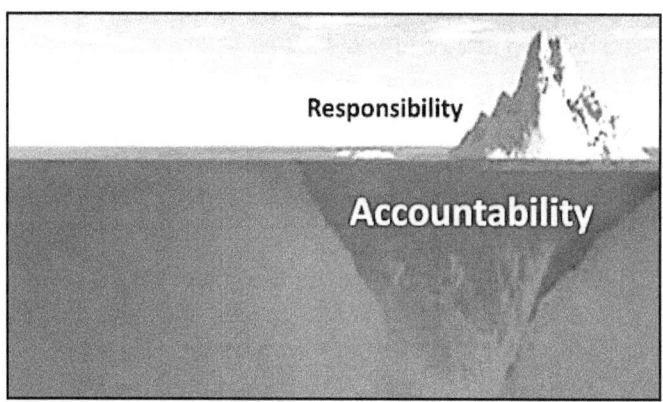

However, you can't see the *accountability* part of the iceberg because it lies hidden beneath the surface until something goes wrong.

What should you do when things go wrong?

When things go wrong for which you're responsible, your boss's job is to ask you for an explanation.

What your boss doesn't need is for you to blame others, make excuses, or hide the truth.

And yes, the mistake may have been made by one of your team members - not you. But your boss doesn't care. He just wants it fixed.

Here's what your boss expects you to do:

Step 1. Step up and accept the blame!

Step 2. Investigate - what happened and what caused it to happen?

Step 3. Report the facts and recommend how it should be fixed.

Step 4. Fix it and fix it for good!

Step 5. When fixed, report the fix to your boss.

Step 6. Make sure it never happens again.

Accountability is something every boss expects from you but won't tell you until it's too late. Unfortunately, this quality isn't something you were born with. And the only time you get to demonstrate your accountability is when things go wrong.

This also includes the actions, in-actions, and adverse consequences of those members within your charge. You're accountable to your boss for everything that happens or fails to happen within your area of responsibility.

However, *accountability* can't exist unless you know all the things for which you're responsible. For example, you can't be held *accountable* for your company's finances if your duties and responsibilities are to service rental cars.

Establish the reputation of being a good problem solver as well as a good problem finder. Your job is to help your boss find and eliminate all the obstacles that could slow or stop achieving his goals.

Remember, mistakes, errors, and defects are not a problem if they're caught and fixed before getting in front of your boss or the customer.

Self-Test
Are you Accountable?

Here are the most important questions to answer to assess your *accountability*.

1. Do you do the right thing?

At an early age, I learned these simple lessons about accountability:

- If you lose, damage, or break something that doesn't belong to you, you need to fix it or buy it.

- If you borrow something, you need to return it in the same or better condition than you found it.

- If you back into and damage someone's car, and they're not around, you need to leave a note on their windshield with your name and phone number to help repair the damage.

- If you were mean or disrespectful to someone, you need to apologize.

2. Are you self-correcting?

A self-correcting person is someone capable of correcting himself without external help.

Part of being *accountable* is being *self-correcting*, especially when starting a new position, even if it's within the same company. Starting anything new is all about learning what you need to know as soon as possible. I'm always amazed by those who never take notes. Why do so few people take notes anymore (with your cell phone or Rocket Book)?

"A short pencil is a long memory." – Unknown.

When you have a question, write it down. Many times, the person with the correct answer won't be immediately available. If you find a term you don't understand, write it down. Later, find out what the term means. Keep a list of all your questions and terms you don't understand. This list will help later when you sponsor a new member into your team. *Self-correcting* people take notes (they don't trust their memory), write down their questions and the answers, and are not afraid to ask questions and proactively seek answers.

3. Do you live your life with no excuses?

People make excuses because it has worked for them in the past. It avoids accepting *accountability*. They're testing your limits to see how much they can get away with, and they fear the consequences of their actions or inactions.

What's the difference between a reason and an excuse?

Here's a simple rule:

Reasons are believable, understandable, and forgivable.

Excuses aren't.

Here are the commonly used excuses:

- **Denial:** Refusing to admit or acknowledge that their behavior is a problem. (Example: "I can stop swearing any time I want. My language isn't that bad.")

- **Isolation:** Removing themselves from the team area to maintain their behavior. (Example: "If I had my own office, this wouldn't be a problem.")

- **Rationalization:** Giving reasons to explain their behavior. (Example: "I screamed at him because he doesn't like me.")

- **Blaming (or Transferal):** Transferring *accountability* for their behavior to others. (Example: "I wouldn't be late all the time if my teammates treated me right.")

- **Projection:** Rejecting their feelings by ascribing them to another (Example: "Why is that stupid idiot so hostile?")

- **Minimizing or Trivialize:** Refusing to admit the effect of their behavior. (Example: "I only told one bad joke. It's not a big deal.")

They close their eyes to the destructive consequences of their unacceptable behavior, or they explain their actions in a way that saves them from having to feel. Either way, it's wrong and must be dealt with immediately.

4. Do you do your best work every day?

Here's a great story about doing your best work.

*It's rumored that when Dr. **Henry Kissinger** was Secretary of State in the administrations of **Presidents Nixon and Ford**, he asked for a security assessment to be made of a foreign country. The first day, when a subordinate delivered the report, Secretary Kissinger asked, "Is this your best work?"*

The subordinate thought for a second and walked out of the office. The second day, the subordinate returned with the report, and Kissinger asked the same question. The subordinate again thought for a moment and walked back out of the office.

On the third day, the subordinate returned, and Kissinger asked for the third time, "Is this your best work?" This time the subordinate said, "Yes." Kissinger then responded, "Good, now I'll read it."

I share this story to highlight that there are no shortcuts to success. Your success will always be linked to *"doing your best work."* Do you do your best work every day? Would your boss agree?

5. Are you proactive?

Another thing that contributes to your effectiveness and success at work is your ability to be proactive.

A proactive person identifies and prevents potential problems by causing things to happen rather than reacting to them after they happen.

Proactive people:

- Identify potential pre-problems before they become a problem and problems before they become a crisis.

- Anticipate their boss's and customer's needs and expectations.

- Use Preventive Actions to identify and resolve all Pre-Problems.

- Take-charge and produce order in the midst of chaos.

- Use collaborative problem solving to build consensus (Chapter 32) and resolve Unresolved Issues.

- Take Immediate Action (Appendix D) and don't wait to be told what to do.

- Anticipate Unintended Consequences and 2d and 3d Order Effects (Appendix F)

- Manage risk and make things happen the right way the first time.

6. Do you make recommendations to your boss to make things better?

Your job is to help your boss achieve his goals. What do you do when you find a problem or an improvement that could make things better? Do you create a *Decision Paper* or a *Business Case* (Appendix E) to make it happen?

I've often written Decision Papers through my boss to his boss because my boss didn't have the funding to make it happen. As shown below, the Decision Paper was addressed "To," my boss's boss, "Thru," my boss.

To: My boss's boss.

Thru: My boss.

From: Me

My boss would then initial and write "Approved" next to the "Thru" line above and send it to his boss for final approval. This process helped my boss move the work forward.

If you cannot answer these questions with a strong YES, you need to reassess your *accountability*. Effective people take this assessment annually and fix what needs to be fixed.

ACKNOWLEDGMENTS

"Many people will walk in and out of your life, but only true friends will leave footprints in your heart."
- Eleanor Roosevelt

I'd like to recognize those with whom I've had the pleasure of serving, whose effectiveness and character I vividly recall, many of whom are not here today to tell their story.

For my military career, I thank Betty McIntee, Edward J. Murphy (my Dad), Dale R. Nelson, Geoffrey "Jeff" Prosch, Craig "Randy" Rutler, Dave Wagner, John Andrews, John "The Bear" Warren, John "Jack" Costello, Dan Labin, and Ron Nicholl for their example of effectiveness.

For my coaching career, I thank Tony Robbins, Bernard Haldane, Jack Bissell, Len Drew, Wayne McCullum, Bob Schrier, John Hurtig, and Bob Gerberg for their mentoring and coaching.

Special thanks to my long-time mentor and friend, Joyce Kuntz, who encouraged me to write this book. After leaving the US Military, Joyce was my first and best boss when I joined her consulting firm in Seattle years ago. Joyce is gone now, but her legacy lives on in this book.

"I must be able to say with sincerity that to see things differently is a strength, not a weakness, in my relationship with others."
- Joyce Kuntz

I thank Joyce's husband, Ed Kuntz, who turned out to be the man who brought me to Seattle from Kansas City to start my incredible second career as an Executive Coach.

And finally, I thank my soulmate and wife, *Diana*, for her love, encouragement, and understanding throughout this process.

When I count my blessings, I always count her twice.

This page is intentionally left blank.

ABOUT THE AUTHOR

"I expect to pass through this world but once; any good thing therefore that I can do, or any kindness that I can show to any fellow creature, let me do it now; let me not defer or neglect it, for I shall not pass this way again."
- Stephan Grelle

Ed Murphy considers himself lucky. From age 7, he knew what he wanted to be when he grew up. He wanted to be a Soldier. After graduating from High School, he joined the US Army and found himself in Basic Training and Advanced Infantry Training at Fort Dix, New Jersey.

A year later, Ed became a Cadet at the United States Military Academy at West Point. In 1970, he graduated as a 2d Lieutenant headed to Airborne and Ranger School, then off to Viet Nam for a year.

In 1978, Ed returned to West Point to teach Military Science and earned an MS from LIU in night school. During his tenure as a Battalion Commander in West Germany, his greatest achievement was helping 1400 soldiers begin a college education. He wanted to give his soldiers something of real value - something that no one could ever take away. After 23 years as a US Army Officer, he retired in 1993.

For his second career, with a little help from *Tony Robbins*, he became an Executive Coach. For the next 21 years, he worked for four of the largest career development and outplacement companies in America, from Seattle, San Diego, Kansas City, and Phoenix.

In 2012, Ed retired a second time and decided to document everything he learned from those he most admired during his 50+ years in the US Military as an Army Officer and Corporate America as an Executive Coach.

In 2014, he began writing books for Amazon and Kindle dedicated to providing the best-in-class wisdom, knowledge, and advice to help others maximize their true career potential by becoming more effective and successful at work and in life.

Today, Ed considers himself blessed to get to live in Phoenix, AZ. He enjoys writing, eating sushi, genealogy, and watching movies with family, friends, and his best friend and wife, ***Diana.***

CONCLUSION

Congratulations!

And thank you for joining us on this *Journey of Discovery*.

As promised, you now have a *Motivational Guide* to add to your professional library - the one I never had.

Every effective boss needs effective followers who can consistently produce excellent results and add value to those who helped produce those results.

You now have the most actionable *Motivational Skills* you were never taught in school or college to support you throughout your career.

Now it's your turn to apply and share this new knowledge to add greater value to your boss and all those with whom you serve.

These are the essential *Best Practices* I've learned over the past 50 years to help you become far more effective and successful than you were yesterday.

As always, I wish you great success.

Never STOP Learning!

Ed

Founder of *The Effectiveness Institute*

email: ed.murphy77@gmail.com

PS: Also, if you feel this information could help someone else, please let them know. If it turns out to make a difference in their life, they'll be forever grateful to you, as will I.

Stop wishing you were better and do something about it today.

www.ingramcontent.com/pod-product-compliance
Lightning Source LLC
Chambersburg PA
CBHW051914170526
45168CB00001B/385